AMERICA AS A MODEL

In memory of Carl Joachim Friedrich

America as a Model

The Impact of American Democracy
in the World

KLAUS VON BEYME
Director, Political Science Institute,
University of Heidelberg

St. Martin's Press   New York

© Klaus von Beyme 1987

Printed in Great Britain
First published in the United States of America in 1987

Library of Congress Cataloging-in-Publication Data

Beyme, Klaus von
  America as a model
  Includes index
  1. United States – Political and government.
2. Democracy. 3 Political participation – United States. 4. Federal government –
United States. 5. Presidents – United States. 6. Judicial review – United States. I.
Title.
JK31.B49 1987   320.473   87-4271

ISBN 0-312-00422-2

Contents

Abbreviations

AEI	American Enterprise Institute
APSR	American Political Science Review
DVA	Deutsche Verlagsanstalt
IPSR	International Political Science Review
JÖR	Jahrbuch für öffentliches Recht
KZfSS	Kölner Zeitschrift für Soziologie und Sozialpsychologie
LGdJ	Librairie générale de droit et de jurisprudence
PVS	Politische Vierteljahresschrift
VVdSTRL	Veröffentlichungen der Vereinigung deutscher Staats-rechtslehrer

Introduction

Since the nineteenth century, democracy has emerged as the most prominent feature of American society, with admirers of America recommending that it be copied and critics of the USA decrying it as the very essence of all that is wrong with the modern world. The influence of the American model, however, was to be found less in democracy in the modern sense of the term, with universal suffrage and the intensive involvement of all ordinary citizens, and more in the constitutional state and the liberal principles of constitutionalism, such as the separation of powers, checks and balances – even within individual powers (such as the bicameral parliament), federalism and the catalogue of guaranteed basic rights.[1] In America, the terms 'democracy' and 'constitutional government' have often been used as synonyms – wrongly so. In the critical appraisal of one of its theoreticians, liberal democracy has been described as 'overwhelmingly liberal and only very tenuously democratic'.[2]

America's exemplary role was to be seen especially in the guarantees set up against possible majority tyranny. The tension between liberalism and democracy has been given an institutionalized form in the American model. In addition, the concept of democracy has been expanded to cover broad areas of society, since an institutionally oriented constitutional discipline never dominated in the USA to the same extent as it did in Europe. This explains why it is no coincidence that the empirical form of political science was able to gain a firm foothold so quickly in America. To begin with, it was still under European influence, partly through emigrants from Europe, such as Francis Lieber, and partly through American researchers who had studied in Europe, such as Arthur F. Bentley. However, it quickly made a break with the institutionalism and normativeness of European constitutional traditions and modelled itself more on the social and behavioural sciences.

The process of the democratization of America since the Jackson era has often been described in terms taken from sociology. There was something of a dearth of constitutional law literature on this subject both in America and in Europe, and the image of America was moulded more by sociological analyses from Tocqueville through to Bryce. Dry treatises on the institutions, such as those presented by Mohl and von Holst in Germany or Rüttimann in Switzerland, only had an influence on specialists. From Mohl right through to Bryce, the writing of such syntheses was repeatedly justified with the argument that American writers had not managed to come up with any 'major syntheses' themselves either.[3] Even the professors of constitutional law themselves had a bad conscience when dealing descriptively with the institutions. At a later date, Mohl described his own work as 'rather poor'.[4] Knowledge of America remained limited among European constitutional academics and, in general, America only appeared as an incidental in constitutional studies, as an arabesque to illustrate contrasts.

This only changed where concern with America was no longer seen as an end in itself and America stood merely as a paradigm for the development of modern societies. In the introduction to his famous book, Tocqueville was already writing: 'For a completely new world, there is a need for a new form of political science.'[5]

Although Tocqueville spoke of 'political science', which at the time did not yet exist as an academic discipline, his book went far beyond the limits of a narrowly defined political science discussion. By the same token, he also made his contribution to sociology and the theory of history. Under his influence, the intellectual occupation with the American model was steered on to a sociological course. It is far from pure chance that there is no other country apart from the USA where sociological jargon has made its way so quickly even into everyday language.[6]

America has been acknowledged as the 'first new nation', characterized by the fundamental values of equality and achievement.[7] Its self-perception has fluctuated between a pioneering role and 'American exceptionalism'. Socio-psychological interpretations, such as those of Riesman or Gorer, tended rather to lay emphasis on America's special role.[8] Macrosociological interpretations, on the other hand, have shown a greater inclination to stress America's paradigmatic role for general trends in the development of civilization.

America often appeared to be not only the 'first new nation state' but also the first modern society with all its advantages and disadvantages. It was far from being a rare assumption that all other modern societies would experience similar developments. The sociologist, Seymour Martin Lipset, put this thesis in a nutshell: 'Thus, at any given time, the differences between America and much of Europe have remained constant, but this difference represented little more than a lagging behind in time.'[9]

An analysis of America's influence in the world must aim to steer a middle course between global sociological analysis and the development of America's historical uniqueness. If America is perceived merely as a pioneer, then borrowings on the American model only represent short-lived catching-up processes, which it is hardly worth studying. For those who regarded America as a completely unique entity in an historicist sense, there was an exotic appeal in researching its history, but parallels with other democracies seemed relatively meaningless. In terms of methodology, political science is otherwise also located between a strongly generalizing, macrosociological approach, looking for laws, and the search for historic uniqueness. Once the general theory of government had basically abandoned comparative analysis, it was political science that had the best access to the institutions which shaped democracy and which at best could only be imitated.

Generally speaking, political science is constituted by the object it deals with. This it shares in part with history and in part with constitutional law but its distinction is that its methodology is predominantly that of social science. Since political science does not have any method unique to itself (like jurisprudence), the result is often less uniform; hence it is no surprise that the 'new political science for a new world' as demanded by Tocqueville should oscillate between the two poles that influenced its genesis.

The extreme sociological oscillation of the nineteenth century led to the whole process of modernization being given the label of 'democracy'. From Mill through to Bryce, Tocqueville has been repeatedly criticized as the originator of this particular view of research into America. As early as 1840, Mill wrote a critique in the *Edinburgh Review*, in which the leading scientific logician branded the crypto-evolutionary traits of Tocqueville's depravation theory in the following terms:

> Tocqueville has, at least apparently, confounded the effects of Democracy with the effects of Civilization. He has bound up in one abstract idea the whole of the tendencies of modern commercial society, and given them one name – democracy.[10]

Even Lord Bryce, who introduced a stricter form of analysis than did

3

Tocqueville, and one more worthy of the name of political science, distanced himself from the famous Frenchman with the comment that he had overestimated democracy and underestimated its institutions.[11]

The importance of the institutions can be seen not only in those aspects of the American model of democracy which have been copied throughout the world but also in the attitude of Americans themselves. Although the sociological approach tends to focus more on the processes of social evolution, and a behaviouralist political science has generally followed sociology in setting priorities, the institutions, especially in America, are certainly not restricted merely to 'grandpa's political science'. Institutions have a particular role to play in America precisely *because* the new nation possessed no established patterns of behaviour or institutions legitimized by tradition. The political institutions rationally and artificially created had a legitimizing force right through to the cult of the American flag, which has repeatedly alienated Europeans: 'The European, who still feels in his bones the whole horror of the fluttering flags of the headlong nationalistic rush into darkness and chaos, feels something of a shiver when he discovers the fuss made over the American flag.'[12] In America, it is sometimes this sort of concrete perception of the institutions that represents stronger points of reference for identification with the political system than is the case in Europe. In a famous comparative study, it emerged that 85 per cent of Americans were proud of their political institutions, compared with 46 per cent of the British, 7 per cent of the Germans and 3 per cent of the Italians.[13] In the ideologically more fragmented landscape of European political cultures, the particular institutions have obviously developed much less power of legitimization than in America. Even in the nineteenth century, Bryce made the observation that the US institutions played a predominant role in America's view of itself without any great outlay on large-scale inquiries. 'What do you think of our institutions?'[14] was what he called a typical American question and one which would hardly ever be asked of a Briton on the Continent. The institutions and national symbols in America acquired their overriding importance precisely because America's political credo remained diffuse and because all-embracing ideological interpretations of the world had little part to play in shaping it. It must also be remembered that the numinous elements of rulers' personalities and dynasties were unable to play the same role as in Europe.

Which institutions are to be seen as most decisive for the American model today? It is only possible to establish criteria to answer this question by adopting a comparative approach. Robert Dahl's classification of the elements of polyarchies is too oriented to the concordant minimum criteria of all democracies (from free elections to the right of association)[15] to permit meaningful distinctions between the American

4

and other models of democracy. Bingham Powell has divided the Western democracies into three groups: 'American and American-dominated', 'British and British-dominated' and 'Continental European' are the government systems he distinguishes. In this typology, the criteria for the American model were the presidential executive and the majoritarian legislature. Outside of America, only the Philippines fitted this type. Strange as it may appear, Japan and the Federal Republic of Germany are counted among the mixed forms. The majoritarian parliament, however, is much more pre-eminent in the British model.[16] These distinctions can be shown to be America-centred and very rough and ready, and they are virtually no use for a detailed description of the unique aspects of the American model.

The characteristics of the American model of democracy appear most clearly when it is contrasted with other government systems. Apart from the agreement method, the differential method must also be used in this type of comparison. The best differentiated model offered to date is that proposed by a Dutch political scientist living in America, Arend Lijphart, who elaborates the differences between majoritarian and consociational democracies. Lijphart's typology shows that the expression 'Anglo-Saxon democracy' used widely but loosely in Europe is misleading. There are similarities between the USA and Great Britain only in three points, intended to produce a government with a majority behind it (concentration of executive power, two-party system and an electoral law based on a relative majority). Measured in terms of other criteria, America is a highly fragmented model – one that was most definitely designed to encourage negotiation with minorities over decisions to be taken (the separation of powers, a bicameral parliamentary system, federalism, a written constitution with built-in barriers making amendments very difficult and judicial review of government and parliamentary decisions).[17] This also shows that the old textbook wisdom regarding the difference between the presidential and parliamentary system has too much of a biased focus on individual institutions. A politico-sociologically oriented analysis of the attitudes and lines of social conflict underlying the institutions will better explain why many countries which remained true to the British Westminster model as regards the organization of the executive and the legislature were still able to borrow from the American model in other areas such as federalism and judicial review.

Of all the criteria for classifying political systems discussed above, the following come in useful for probing those areas where the American model of democracy has been most influential, and they thus form the basis of the present analysis:

1   the presidential system (Chapter 2)

2   federalism (Chapter 3)

3   judicial review (Chapter 4).

In addition, individual institutions in the area of

4   representation and participation (Chapter 5) have been im-
     portant for constitutionalism throughout the world.

5   Finally, the view of the American model has changed as a re-
     sult of the United States foreign-policy role as a world power,
     which makes it necessary to look at the links between the
     world-power role, the concept of 'mission' and the future of
     the American model (Chapter 6).

In the limited space available, brevity is of the essence. That is why
no attempt will even be made to look into all the aspects of the
American image. This work has already been done in numerous detailed investigations into individual countries and periods. All that can
be done here is to discuss the most influential studies on the American
image. The emphasis is not placed on the incidental opinions of individual travellers and theoreticians, who more or less dominate the literature on the subject. What is primarily under consideration here is the
actual influence exerted by the American model of democracy on the
processes of adoption and the drawing up of constitutions throughout
the world.

An attempt to find the real influences cannot always take verbal references to the American model at face value. On very many occasions
it can be shown that foreign theoreticians and politicians were only
looking for functional equivalents when they referred to the USA. In
the area of political influences, it is also far from easy to arbitrate in the
long-standing ethnological conflict between diffusionists and func-
tionalists. Have institutions formed as a reaction to similar challenges
within different societies or have they been spread by diffusion? As
long as America was unable to make use of force to bring about the
dissemination of its model, there is more to be said for the explanation
of numerous borrowings from the American model as being the search
for functional equivalents. Ever since Calhoun, the temptation to
spread American democracy by making use of the very military means
that contradict the fundamental principles on which it is founded has
quite rightly been seen not as one of the available options but as more of
a threat.

Notes

1   Ronald G. Landes: *The Canadian Polity. A Comparative Introduction*, Scarborough/Ontario, Prentice Hall, Canada, 1983, p. 98.
2   Andrew Levine: *Liberal Democracy. A Critique of Its Theory*, New York, Columbia PU, 1981, p. 7.
3   Robert von Mohl: *Das Bundesstaatsrecht der Vereinigten Staaten von Nordamerika. Erste Abteilung. Verfassungsrecht*, Stuttgart, 1824; James Bryce: *The American Commonwealth (1888)*, New York, Putnam, 1959, Vol. 1, p. 5.
4   Robert von Mohl: *Lebenserinnerungen*, Stuttgart, DVA, 1902, Vol. 2, pp. 260 ff.
5   Alexis de Tocqueville: *De la démocratie en Amérique*, Paris, Gallimard (*Oeuvres complètes*, Vol. 1), 1962, Vol. 1, p. 5.
6   Ralf Dahrendorf: *Die angewandte Aufklärung. Gesellschaft und Soziologie in Amerika*, Frankfurt, Fischer, 1968, pp. 12 ff.
7   Seymour M. Lipset: *The First New Nation. The United States in Historical and Comparative Perspective*, Garden City, Anchor Book, (1963) 1967, p. 2.
8   David Riesman: *The Lonely Crowd*, New Haven, Yale UP, 1950; Geoffrey Gorer: *The American People*, New York, 1948; Max Lerner: *America as a Civilization*, New York, Schuster & Simon, 1957, pp. 64 ff.
9   Lipset, op. cit. p. 148.
10 John. S. Mill: *M. de Tocqueville and Democracy in America. Dissertations and Discussions*, London, 1859, Vol. 2, p. 62.
11 Bryce, op. cit. Vol. 1, p. 4.
12 Gabriel A. Almond/Sidney Verba: *The Civic Culture*, Princeton UP, 1963, p. 102.
13 Paul Watzlawick: *Gebrauchsanweisung für Amerika*, Munich, Piper, 1984, 8th Edition, p. 146.
14 Bryce, op. cit., Vol. 1, p. 1.
15 Robert A. Dahl: *Dilemmas of Pluralist Democracy*, New Haven, Yale UP, 1982, pp. 10 f.
16 G. Bingham Powell Jr.: *Contemporary Democracies*, Cambridge/Mass, Harvard UP, 1982, p. 67.
17 Arend Lijphart: *Democracies. Patterns of Majoritarian and Consensus Government in Twenty-One Countries*, New Haven, Yale UP, 1984, pp. 33 ff.

1 The Evolving Image of America: from Republic to Democracy

Negative perceptions of the American image

To begin with, it was Republicans who were more interested in America as a model. The republic, which had deteriorated to the level of a form of government only classified in the pages of textbooks and at best still appeared to be alive only in remote places such as the Swiss mountains, suddenly awoke to a new lease of life in America. It was only when the concept of 'democracy' began to be superimposed on that of 'republic' as the basic analytical term that other groups also began to take an interest in America as a model.

In its early years the American image had to contend with three main accusations:

1   a number of writers played it up as an improved England.

2   with the French Revolution, America was seen in many quarters as France's precursor and source of inspiration.

3   and finally, America had a purely functional role imposed on it as part of the party wrangling between pro-French and pro-English groupings, and was not understood in its own right.

1   To begin with, the image of America suffered both ways – either through the view that it was 'an underdeveloped New England' or through the diametrically opposed view that it contained the seeds for a

new and better England, which would contrast strongly with the rotten old one. The French Enlightenment's search for the 'state in its true primeval condition' had concentrated primarily on the eastern part of Asia. Now it became customary among a faction of European Radicals to see it in America, and Americans had the advantage that they represented something more than being extremely and exotically different in ways which appeared incomprehensible in Europe. Richard Price's generalizations are typical of this attitude and he shows exactly the same spirit as Rousseau.

Price regarded the middle course between savagery and civilization as the happiest stage for mankind, which in America's case, however, ran the risk of being corrupted as a result of too much trade with Europe. The American yeomanry was pitched against the British mercantile spirit:

> From one end of North America to the other they are fasting and praying. But what are we doing? – Shocking thought! we are rediculing (sic) them as Fanatics, and scoffing at religion . . . Here we see an old state, great indeed, but inflated and irreligious, enervated by luxury, encumbered with debts; and hanging by a thread.[1]

Liberal Whig philosophy, on the other hand, saw England in a more favourable light than did the radicalism of a non-conformist minister like Richard Price. It was for political reasons (and not social ones) that conservative observers were not ready to transfigure the 'new Barbarians'. It happened not infrequently that for social reasons Americans were also compared with the 'uncouth Russians' – this was very much a one-way process, and Marx polemicized against it at an early stage in a letter to his Russian translator.[2] As this sort of comparison was being made, it was not long before prophesies emerged as to the future world-power role of what are today's Superpowers.[3]

The image of a Transatlantic Arcadia (regardless of whether a good or bad interpretation was placed on it) collapsed between Jackson's movement for more democracy and the Civil War. In the Old World it became all the rage to talk about profit greed, closed sects, corruption and uninhibited individualism and America was not spared the comparison with Russia even in these negatively interpreted traits. Conservative organicists and circulatory theoreticians later pushed the parallels to extremes and refused to concede that America actually had any real period at its prime between its ascendancy and its decay. When it came to the primacy of economics, the dictatorship of public opinion and state capitalism, cultural pessimists, such as Spengler and Keyserling, went so far as to draw a comparison with Soviet Russia.[4] Even the positive identification of similarity produced some strange offshoots during the Second World War: no other than the Webbs suddenly saw the Soviet Union as the 'most inclusive and equalized democracy in the world',[5] not with a view to doing America down but in order to declare the Soviet Union as of equal birth to the USA.

America reacted to the unappreciative commentaries which began with John Adams by declaring that European travellers and journalists demonstrated 'complete ignorance',[6] and later historical investigations carried out in Europe itself confirmed this verdict.[7] It was necessary to have spent at least a decade in America like the Austrian nobleman, Francis Grund, to be in a position to paint a fair picture of the country, one which was clouded neither by American inferiority complexes nor by European arrogance.:

> When I thus speak of American politicians, I do not mean to draw envious comparisons between them and European statesmen. I belong neither to that class of European that cannot pronounce the name of America without a grudge, nor to that class of fashionable and travelled American that cannot find anything in their own country equal to Europe. On the contrary, I maintain that there is quite as much intelligence, application, and certainly of virtue, in the members of the cabinet at Washington, as can be found in the ministerial council of any European prince. And I say this, fully aware of its producing more sneers among the higher classes in America than in Europe.[8]

Such views stood healthily apart from the idyllic reports of those travellers who claimed to have seen the American President tethering his own horse in front of the White House and who came to America 'without any prior knowledge but ready to admire the democratic institutions' – as one English traveller put it. However, they also stand apart from those critics who claim to have found unruliness and terror in the House of Representatives inhibiting the Opposition.[9]

2   In the period after the French Revolution, attitudes towards the events that had occurred became the central point of controversy among the emerging parties in Europe, and from then on, America was often seen as being only the precursor or source of inspiration for the events in France. Although Lafayette originally went to America more for reasons of ambition, frustration and Anglophobia than love of freedom, he also played an enthusiastic part in establishing the legend of two revolutions in a single spirit,[10] even though there was soon to be a conflict of interests between the two countries. Patriots handed the key to the Bastille over to Washington through Thomas Paine in order to give more weight to the myth of a common revolution. Conservative theoreticians of the policy that opposed the French Revolution also tried to denounce American connivance during the period of the Revolution. A comment by Friedrich Schlegel may be taken to typify this attitude:

It is actually probably unjust to call this Revolution only a French one or to regard it solely as such. It was a political disease, an epidemic affecting whole peoples at the time . . . The true nursery of all these destructive principles, the revolutionary training ground for France and the rest of Europe had been North America.[11]

Despite the extent to which radical British writers such as Paine and Price also propagated this myth, it was something not all Americans were ready to believe of themselves. The American reaction to the French Revolution was a perfectly independent one and it was soon to be characterized by the emerging self-interests of the American parties. It is true that the Federalists in America were also in favour of freedom and a republic but they certainly had their reservations. For a time, France had the effect of driving people into one party or another, whereas it is not possible to conclude that the opposite was also true. Washington and Hamilton maintained American neutrality throughout the revolutionary wars. The Federalists, however, were at heart pro-English, while the Anti-Federalists tended rather to be a pro-French party. Burke's 'Reflections' and Paine's 'Rights of Man' became sources of inspiration for the formulation of party attitudes on the French Revolution. By the very latest as of the end of the Revolution in France, as a result of Napoleon's *coup d'état*, even Jefferson was attaching higher priority to national self-interest than to party preferences based more on emotion.

Equating the American and the French Revolutions was not something that all Americans were ready to go along with and it also became subject to increasing criticism in Europe. Liberals, who had welcomed the American Revolution, became the embittered opponents of the French. Burke was the incarnation of this ideological shift. Radicals such as Joseph Priestley did not understand this turnabout, as can be seen from a letter he wrote to Burke: 'That an avowed friend of the American Revolution should be an enemy of that of the French, which arose from the same general principles, and in a great measure sprung from it, is to me unaccountable.'[12]

Burke had been one of the first to realize that the American Revolution had much more in common with the defence of long-established English freedoms than the holistic rationalism of the French Jacobins had in common with French principles. The American Revolution *was* compatible with the newly-defined principles of conservatism, the French was not. Burke's admirers on the continent also refused to equate the two revolutions. Friedrich Gentz, who was later to become a brilliant writer in Metternich's service, provided a clear distinction between the two revolutions as early as 1800:

In the course of the American Revolution, human rights were never put forward as a reason for destroying the rights of the population. The sovereignty of the people was never used as a pretext to undermine the rule of law or the fundamentals of security within society; it was never admitted that an individual, or even a whole class of individuals, or even more so the representatives of one estate or another were invoking the Declaration of Rights in order to escape positive commitments or to pay lip-service to obeying the popular sovereign. Finally, it never occurred to a legislator or statesman in America to challenge the legality of the constitutions of foreign states and to present the American Revolution as a model for any other people or as the dawn of a completely new epoch for civilized society.[13]

Conservatives also began to make an increasing distinction between the two revolutions. Somewhat weaker words started to be applied to the American movement, such as 'rebellion', 'insurrection', 'insolence' or 'war'.[14] The Liberals, on the other hand, placed more emphasis on the revolutionary character of the American movement for independence but at the same time praised its moderation:

> It is a decisive feature of this revolution and of the Teutonic national character that the final decision was brought about less through battles and a rapid succession of blows than through a durable organized system of resilient and passive resistance.[15]

Even in the constitutional terminology preferred in liberal and enlightened circles, the distinction was thus explained less in terms of political principles and more in terms of differences between Germanic and Latin races. In the case of America, these admirers also praised the absence of a missionary spirit, which was contrasted with the sufferings endured by the neighbouring states as a consequence of the French Revolutionary Wars.

In Germany, enthusiasm for America resulted in part from opposition to 'Perfidious Albion', which had become the world's leading economic power. Contrary to attitudes on France, pro-Americanism had virtually no consequences. An American observer came to the conclusion that: 'The strong terms used by political writers to show their enthusiasm for the Republican cause and their hatred of tyranny were on the whole mere day-dreaming. No one really thought (. . .) of overturning conditions in Germany.' In the case of Belgium, a similar passive stance was justified in terms of the lack of support from outside.[16]

Historians writing about the American Revolution later had more detailed knowledge available to them than did contemporary journalists. They, however, also failed to agree on the question of the revolutionary character of the American independence movement and the question was often decided as a function of the individual's own political standpoint. Conservative observers from Bancroft through to Rossiter have tended to come down against the assumption of a revolution. Emphasis was placed on the fundamental consensus amongst

Americans, which led to the paradox that, although the Revolution was 'extremely radical in nature', it was 'brought about with such benign tranquillity that even conservatism hesitated to censure.'[17]

Historiographers of later years have tried to decide this problem of judgement empirically. In his classic work, *The Age of the Democratic Revolution*, R.K. Palmer submitted factual evidence in favour of the revolutionary nature of the movement. His argument was that, in per capita terms, more people had emigrated from America and more property had been confiscated than in France, in other words, the extent of the social upheaval occasioned by the American Revolution had been underestimated.[18] Marxists do not have the slightest problem either in recognizing the American independence movement as a 'bourgeois revolution'. Such honours, however, were only granted *ex post facto*. They had no real consequences and it was for other reasons that America came to be admired in Europe, by conservatives as well. Hannah Arendt and others praised the American Revolution especially because it had not only changed society. Among the innovations, particular emphasis was placed on what left-wingers readily disparaged as the 'carry-over phenomenon': the new political order which was celebrated precisely because of its inheritance of Aristotelean thought. The fact that the new order began by creating a constitution is hardly such a unique event as Dolf Sternberger and others before him assume. Even the October Revolution led to a constitution, but all other revolutionary constitutions had neither the same relative degree of importance in the new system nor the same permanence as the American Constitution. The mere politico-liberal solution has perhaps also been exaggerated. Psychologists have spoken heartlessly of the 'Jefferson Swindle', couched as the right to the 'pursuit of happiness' in the Declaration of Independence drafted by Jefferson. In a less liberal society, the eschatological characteristic so despised by European liberal conservatives could have made its way into politics as a consequence of such formulations. Although Hannah Arendt construes aspects of 'communal happiness' in this form of words, it is worth noting that in America the formula for happiness is still predominantly perceived in the sense of 'possessive individualism' and, contrary to France, no *comité du salut public* was set up, the final effect of which was that the concept of happiness led to benevolent dictatorship. Present-day psychologists also interpret the typical American idea of the right to happiness in purely individual terms.[19]

What we are concerned with here is the influence of the American model, not a reconstruction of factual developments; that is why on this particular question it is the subjective view of contemporary journalists and theorists which, by way of exception, is more important than the actual social upheavals. It remains a fact that, thanks to the more detailed knowledge in Europe regarding the degree of violence in France and the moderation with which the political experiment was conducted in America, both Liberals and Conservatives in other countries were able to accept the American Revolution but could only reject the French.

3   The functional use to which the American image was put was a consequence of the fact that attitudes in Europe to the USA did not have any polarizing effect. Advocates and opponents of the French Revolution had a fixation for France, and they rarely mentioned America. The French Revolution was the central issue which divided Liberals and Conservatives in Europe. In France itself, the Restoration ushered in a new pro-American wave. America was used as the legitimization for the republican idea which had been vanquished in France. Both camps, however, were thinking primarily of France and they were really struggling intellectually over the true position of their own revolution whenever they discussed America. Tocqueville pulled no punches when he admitted as much in the preface to his famous book: 'I admit that in America I was looking for more than America. . . I was wanting to think about the future.'[20]

America first began to be considered to some extent as a subject in its own right with the process of democratization under Jackson. A type of textbook democracy (one which appeared not to have been in real existence since ancient times) won a new lease of life. A number of authors compared the Attic and American democracies.[21] Liberal authors went so far as to stress that it was in America that the first true democracy came into being – even if it was still just a 'fledgling':

> Since the Republics of ancient times were more democratic by name than in practice, given that, apart from the fact that they were based on the slavery of the majority of their population, they all permitted their citizens to be divided into several classes.[22]

From this point of view it was the 'equality' of all citizens which first made for a genuine democracy. With the development of a more radical view of democracy among Socialists, the democratic nature of the American model was once again called into question. In polemic writings right up to the present, it is a favourite trick to quote the anti-democratic utterances of many of the founding fathers.[23] Compared with America's own self-apotheosis as a democracy 'built on a natural foundation', a certain scepticism had long been present in academic circles. It was above all between democracy and puritanism, with the latter's emphasis on the sovereignty of God and the doctrine of predestination, that there was, to begin with, no affinity at all. Despite this, a religion which placed a Bible in the hands of every believer was subsequently to facilitate the 'unification of a Puritan conversionist

movement and democratic enlightenment'.[24] Not even the purest
propaganda rhetoric would still claim today that the founding fathers
were democrats in the modern sense. In the American model of constitutionalism, everything that could lead to concentration of power was
avoided. The aim was neither the British parliamentary system nor continental Rousseauism.[25] The American system was seen as a variation
on the British, the differences being justified by the system itself; hence
it was merely a system that had set itself the target of ironing out the
supposed degenerations of the Westminster model, such as the cabinet
system and the type of political parties. In this somewhat strange approach to adopting certain institutions from the British model, what
was overlooked was the fact that some had actually long since been regarded as out-of-date in Great Britain itself, such as the head of state's
right of veto and the incompatibility between ministerial office and a
parliamentary mandate, which had been relaxed since the Regency Act
of 1706.

It was precisely these conservative traits in American constitutionalism which made the model so quickly acceptable to relatively conservative groups abroad. Despite all the criticism of 'Jacksonian democracy'
and advancing egalitarianism, conservative sources praised the fact
that the ancient commonplace that democracy would tend towards mob
rule (ochlocracy) had not, in fact, been fulfilled. Why it should be that
the degeneration into ochlocracy inherent in a democratic form of
government did not actually occur, was usually explained by the fact
that the populace was not strong enough to band together, given the
harsh living conditions in an agricultural country and, whenever 'pressure from the streets' seemed to be building up, there was always the
safety valve of moving further westwards as a means of alleviating such
pressure. Sometimes the helpless fate of the population at large was
commented on in downright cynical terms, as by the German historian,
Heinrich von Treitschke:

> Just consider the most charming mob existing anywhere in the world –
> that of New York. It represents the accumulated rejects of the whole
> world, and yet, see how these depraved social elements, left to their own
> devices, are forced to pull themselves together here. Do you really be-
> lieve that even a Prussian police force could hold them in such bounds as
> they are kept in by the stringent law of dire necessity. Here, everyone
> knows full well whether I am dying of hunger, which is why nobody
> cares.[26]

Such cynicism has not entirely disappeared. A milder form still exists
in a variation which claims that the welfare state is hastening the degeneration of democracy by increasing expectations.

Reducing American events to the function of paving the way for the
French Revolution, and functionalizing America for the purposes of

15

party conflicts which formed as a result of attitudes on the French Revolution and not the American, has been seen as the consequence of a number of shifts which began with the French Revolution, saw their justification in German idealism and were given the final touch by Marxism.[27] An analysis that deals with more than the excursions in philosophical utterances on America will have to make a sharper distinction between different nations, periods of time and party political groupings.

The periods of influence of American democracy

In examining the accusations against the American image it has become clear that this went through a process of evolution, with pro and anti-American stances represented by different groups at different periods of time. These groups reacted less to happenings in America itself than to events in Europe, particularly in times of revolutionary turmoil, such as 1789, 1830, 1848 and 1917/18. Only two events in American history came in for such a degree of attention as to modify the parties' image of America:

1   the Jacksonian democracy

2   and the American Civil War.

Carl J. Friedrich has distinguished three periods of the American image:

1   the period of widespread sympathy for America,

2   a middle period, which reached its culmination in 1848 and which led to a wave of adoption of American institutions,

3   and a late phase since the First World War, when authoritarian regimes collapsed and models were needed for the process of democratization.[27]

On the whole, this division is a perfectly serviceable one, even in the light of a detailed study of history. In a number of countries there were, however, other turning points, which would make a subdivision of these long-term cycles seem appropriate. In France, for instance, 1830 would represent one such turning point.

1   As regards the *period of the French Revolution*, it is impossible to agree with Friedrich when he assesses it as a 'period of general en-

16

thusiasm' for the American model. As a model, France carried much greater influence. In Italy, it was copied fairly slavishly. Even the Spaniards' pride in their democratic Constitution of Cádiz, dating from 1812, cannot conceal the fact that many passages were culled virtually verbatim from the French Constitution of 1791. There was no lack of complaints among Spanish Conservatives about the exaggerated *'francesismo'*, although some of the leading orators, such as Argüelles, believed they were actually reestablishing 'Spain's original constitution'[28] – a recurring theme in many attempts at adoption. North America played only a minor role in the creation of the constitutional monarchies, since, right up into the nineteenth century, an existential distinction was made between constitutional monarchy and representative democracy. It was only in the 1830s, when the concept of a 'representative system' and the way it functioned with the preponderance of parliament became a sort of generic term, that material differences in forms of government began to lose significance.

In the period of restoration the American Republic was important as a model only for groups in opposition. The lack of influence exerted by republicans in the Europe of the Holy Alliance rendered the idealization of America devoid of content. The image of America started to change in 1830, beginning in France. Lafayette was no longer the unchallenged hero of two different nations, and the number of travellers to America and the knowledge of that land both increased. More subtle distinctions were made within the American image. Subsequent to the Jacksonian democracy, the view of a virtuous, agricultural Arcadia on the other side of the Atlantic became sullied by elements of a mercantile, profit-oriented society. The liberal groups, which increased their influence in France after 1830, were now only ready to accept some of the American institutions and the liberalism behind them but not the society, the *'moeurs publiques'*, or the trends towards an egalitarian democracy. The 'party squabbles' and 'economic nepotism' in America became a focal point for criticism. The widespread denunciation of parties was based on a traditional belief in consensus and could thus find no example worth following in America. It was rare indeed for the critics to adopt such a moderate tone as one German constitutional lawyer, who saw the parties as having the positive function of 'mitigating the autocratic rule of the people' within the American 'representative democracy', while at the same time attempts were made to keep the European constitutional monarchies free of this American party spirit.[29] The increase in racial conflict also sullied the image of the USA. A fragmented society with a confusing abundance of racial, ethnic, religious and class conflicts did not fit the progressive image of the French *'volonté générale'* or the concept of a *'nation une et indivisible'* (single, indivisible nation), which was increasingly being accepted by

French conservatives as well once daydreams about restoring the estate-structured *ancien régime* had faded to mere illusion.

With the Civil War, theories on the depravity of America found an increasing number of people in Europe ready to believe them. Even a Swiss Radical, such as Rüttimann, dwelt at length in his monumental work on negative phenomena like the falling level of education, the vulgarization of the English language, the political conflicts, the weakening of family bonds and the pursuit of wealth and pleasure. Unlike Tocqueville, Mill and Mohl ('eminent thinkers of a genuinely liberal persuasion'), Rüttimann was not ready to ascribe these simply to democracy, as was the fashion of the time, he saw them as determined by uniquely American events such as the buffetings of the revolution and the rapid expansion of North America into the South and West.[30] The acceptance of the sociological criticism (coupled with leniency in the evaluation of the political institutions), which, especially for someone from Switzerland, had the additional advantage of not discrediting democracy *per se*, was a ploy widely used in literature from Laboulaye through to Bryce.

2   It was during the *period of the 1848 Revolution* that Europe first started to borrow more heavily from the American model – nowhere (apart from Latin America) was there any question of total identification, there was only the creation of functional equivalents on the basis of independent constitutional traditions. In many countries the parties began to take on a more definite shape than the pre-1848 ideological groupings which were largely organized in the light of their attitude towards the French Revolution. More than ever before, the American image was brought into the service of party programmes, but these were focused on Europe and not based on discriminating knowledge of America. Nonetheless, individual protagonists, such as Tocqueville and Beaumont in the French Constitutional Committee, Rüttimann in Switzerland and Mohl in the German *Paulskirche* Parliament, were able to incorporate their profound knowledge of America into the political decision-making processes, and the parties' views on America suddenly found themselves subject to rapid change:

(i)   'The *Liberals*, who in many countries formed the first modern party, became more critical vis-à-vis America. The enthusiasm for America expressed in Rotteck's and Welcker's liberal '*Staatslexikon*' no longer had any adequate equivalent in the *Paulskirche* Parliament. The Liberals in the French National Assembly around 1848 were clearly divided. A parliamentary study showed that seven Liberals spoke in favour of the American model and nine Liberals against it.[31]

(ii)   On the one hand, the *conservatives* had become more composed in their judgement of the American model born of a revolution, than they had been at the time of the French Revolution, when the American freedom movement was often accused of connivance. On the other hand, they were even more enthusiastic than the Liberals in espousing a belief in the theories of degeneration and fear of democracy that were increasingly emerging from this preoccupation with America. It was only the militant Legitimists, whose whole approach was based on the dichotomy between republic and monarchy, who were unable to glean anything from the USA's republican model. Once, Chateaubriand, one of the founders of theoretical and practical conservatism in France, went so far in his memoirs as to express the belief that the issue of the definitive form of government had not been finally decided even in America. However, he abstained from making detailed forecasts and sought to escape by drawing daring parallels with Ancient Rome, of the sort that only became widespread once America had actually become a world power. America's westward expansion was compared with Rome's expansion northwards and consequences for the form of government were then read into it: 'Once the Roman Republic crossed the Alps (. . .) it turned into a monarchy.'[32]

In Germany, Hegel held similar conservative ideas, whereby a state would have to go through a 'maturing process' first before being ready for monarchy. Speaking of North America, Hegel commented that the state 'had not yet advanced far enough to have a need for monarchy.'[32]

The old tenet of constitutional doctrine that democracies were only possible in small states had persisted obstinately for a long time, laying emphasis on the Swiss example, although the American model increasingly gave it the lie.

In 1848, the question as to which form of government played a certain role in the adoption of the directly elected president (cf. Chapter 3), since conservative liberals, who had been supporters of the Orleanist system, were forced to look to America in their search for as close a republican image of constitutional monarchy as possible. Tocqueville and his friends became the 'pro-American party *par excellence*' since they felt no affection for the Legitimist President, Henri V, and the Orleanist system had been such a short-lived experiment anyway that they were ready to come to terms with the republic. The American President as a substitute king, a bicameral system and power of veto for the head of the executive to mitigate the effects of government by democratic majority were the trump cards this group had in its hand.

(iii)   In many countries, *Radicals* and *Socialists* began by being positively inclined towards the American model. When Mittermaier held his ardently pro-American speech in the Frankfurt *Paulskirche* in 1848 the applause and cheering came only from the left.[33] In France as well, there was a repetition of the scenes of fraternization between the Left and America in 1848. The American Ambassador, Richard Rush, had recognized the provisional government of the Second Republic without receiving instructions from Washington. On 28 February he made his way to the *Hotel de Ville* and addressed the provisional government, whilst the people assembled outside chanted: '*Vive la Republique des États-Unis!*' ('Long live the American Republic!').[34] President Polk subsequently endorsed this autonomous step taken by the American representative in France and Secretary of State James Buchanan informed Rush of the decision and also issued all sorts of good advice for the new Republic. As in 1789, American politicians showed a degree of concern over the French custom of romanticizing about the barricades. The instructions contained a warning against revolutionary wars and the advice to adopt the federal system.[35] These warnings fitted nicely with the conservative image that even Italian radicals were gaining at the time. To their surprise, American politicians showed little enthusiasm for republics brought into being as a result of fighting on the barricades.[36]

In 1848 it was obvious on many occasions that the rhetoric that could be summoned up to evoke the idea of common republican ideals, which had played an important part on public platforms early on, had become virtually exhausted. Apart from initial enthusiasm over the American encouragement, the Left had not recognized America as an example to follow. There was a very deeply rooted prejudice that the American model was only valid for federal states; federalism, however, was incompatible with the Jacobin idea of the '*nation une et indivisible*'. In the constitutional debates, a minority of ten left-wing members spoke out in favour of the American model, while a majority group of eleven spoke against it.[37] That is still lumping Radicals and Socialists together. The result thus conceals the fact that the Socialists within the Left tended to harbour even greater reservations concerning American Constitutionalism than did the Radical Republicans.

The times had gone when America represented something positive for early Socialists in the form of a rich experimental terrain for radical religious and political sects, where visions of socialism could be tried out on a small scale. The image of a boundlessly acquisitive society also began to superimpose itself on the communard idyll among socialists. Marx and Engels, who made the most decisive claims to have transformed socialism from a utopia to a science, were also the most resolute in putting the transfigurative interpretation of images of agricultural communes in America straight.

For Marx and Engels, America was the country where capitalism was increasing at a rapid pace. Until the time of the Civil War, America's economy was often still interpreted as an adjunct of European capitalism. Marx was one of the first to make economic growth (and not the consequential social phenomena) the basis of his analysis. Overhasty capitalist development could theoretically also have meant an increase in the revolutionary working class. Marx and Engels, however, remained ambivalent on this particular point. The transfer of the *Internationale* cannot be taken as belief in America as a revolutionary model, it was a tactical move to get rid of internal opponents within Europe as part of the factional infighting.[38] The assessment of America's revolutionary potential was ambivalent, based on the experience that many European socialists lost their radicalism after crossing the Atlantic. In 1891, Engels wrote to Joseph Weydemeyer in Zürich:

> Moreover, there is a lot still to be done in New York and we are seriously lacking a regular representative of our Party there, someone who also has theoretical training. You will find a sufficient number of elements but your biggest single hindrance will be that the Germans with potential, ones who have a certain value, tend to Americanize easily and to drop any intention of returning; and then, of course, there are the particular American circumstances to be considered: the ease with which excess population can be drained off into the countryside, and the essential acceleration in the country's prosperity, which make the bourgeois lifestyle seem like a *beau idéal* to them.[39]

Much to Marx's and Engels' regret, 'Americanism' often became a surrogate for socialism.[40] Marx fought indefatigably against Americanism and the view that bourgeois society could be developed without class struggles – an idea put forward by C. H. Carey, whom he went so far as to describe as the 'only significant North American economist'. But to begin with, Marx still explained the absence of class conflict in terms of the underdeveloped nature of the country: 'Of course, all he demonstrates is that, for him, the "underdeveloped" conditions in the United States count as "normal conditions".'[41]

The faster America developed, the more it fulfilled his own forecasts as regards social consequences. The central problem with Marx's analysis, however, remained the fact that 'a class *per se*' (the objective existence of social classes) developed even less than in Europe into 'a class *pro se*' (i.e. subjective class consciousness).[42] In a speech to the General Council in 1872, Marx cited the USA as being the only country where, apart from Great Britain (and out of politeness he added Holland, since the meeting was taking place in The Hague), the possibility of a peaceful transition to Socialism was not entirely ruled out. He did not, however, see this transition as being free of conflict either. In opposition to the Henry George Movement, any attempt to deny the growth of class antagonisms in America was repeatedly challenged.[43]

After Marx's death, Engels was forced to dampen increasing revolutionary expectations on several occasions. In 1881, he noted that American workers were still not ready to read Socialist literature.[44] In 1886, he explained this in terms of 'difficult learning processes':

> In such a naturally evolved land as America, which has developed as a purely bourgeois one without any feudal past but, in the process, has nonetheless taken over from England many aspects of an ideology remaining from feudal times, to wit: English common law, religion, sectarianism, and where the basic necessities of the practical worker and the concentration of capital has engendered a general despising of all things theoretical which is only now going astray in the most educated classes of academics – and in such a country people must come to recognize their own social interests by bitter first-hand experience. It is something the workers will not be spared either; the confusion of Trades Unions, Socialists, Knights of Labor, etc. will continue for some time to come, and they will only learn the hard way. The main thing, however, is that they have now started to move, that progress is being made at all, that the spell has been broken, and that things will move quickly, more quickly than anywhere else, even if in a distinctive way and one which may appear almost crazy from the theoretical point of view.[45]

Such attempts at self-appeasement did not always sound convincing. Engels placed his hopes in zigzag movements, whereby, after quietistic periods, the revolutionary climaxes would be all the more concentrated.[46] Whereas it had once been the rapid Americanization of European emigrants that was held responsible for setbacks, it was now the leaders of the party and the trades unions, some of whom had been born in Europe, who were accused of a lack of ability to grasp what was required in America. It was above all the Germano-American socialists, who, according to Engels, had allowed Marx's theory to degenerate into rigid orthodoxy. That is why they remained mere sects and, as Hegel put it, 'they will get from nowhere, through nowhere to nowhere'.[47] Above all else, Engels warned against premature experiments with third parties and thereby showed a certain insight into the operation of the system.

The ambivalent attitudes towards America, hovering between criticism and hope, was widespread in left-wing circles. It was only with Sombart's explanation as to why there was no socialism in America that the hopes of the workers' movement on the continent for a revolutionary development in America finally ceased.[48] Anyone who accepts as valid Lowi's[49] subsequent explanation for the 'non-happening of a socialist movement', i.e., the fragmentation of the country as a result of federalism, will regard the socialists as well-advised even in those days in their aversion to too much federalism. By nature, they were less interested in federalism, checks and balances and judicial review than were the bourgeois theoreticians. There was, however, a pro-Americanism, especially among German left-wing thinkers, which lasted well into the days of the USPD (Independent Social Democratic Party, 1917-22). It was only at the end of the First World War that this entered a period of crisis to the same extent as anti-Americanism among the right wing in Germany abated.[50] This positive view of America held by left-wingers did not, however, have any impact, since (with the exception of Italy and France) the influence of socialists was relatively limited in nearly every country until 1917. In that year the extreme Left's search for a model turned eastwards and Russia became the model. Only indirectly did some of the red glow cast its light on America – in the form of a few words of praise uttered by Lenin, who went so far as to justify adopting the American Taylor system.[51]

It is also true that there was a turn away from America among the moderate Left, which did not accept the Soviet model. This was largely a result of the disappointment over the failure of Wilson's New Order policy and neo-isolationism – facts, which, on the other hand, tended rather to please the Right. A complete reversal in the image of America began, and this was a trend which was to reach its climax after the Second World War.

After the hopes of 1848 and the new systems had collapsed (as early as 1849 in Germany and 1851 in France), America then had very little influence as a model on the drafting of later constitutions. This applies to both the German Empire set up in 1871 and the Third French Republic. The War of Secession had cast a shadow on the Left's image of America. The 'ugly American' was not the result they had promised themselves from their support for Lincoln and the North. The shock of the heavy losses in the Civil War was felt even in Switzerland, which had also just gone through a civil war, but one of more 'humane' dimensions. It was with absolute abhorrence that the 78 lives lost in the Swiss Civil War of 1847 were contrasted in Swiss literature with the half a million deaths in the American Civil War.[52] It was not until after the First World War, when many states began to reconstitute themselves, that once again discussions of the American model had a real political impact.

3   Whereas *after the First World War* the influences of the American model of democracy had been only indirect, after the Second World War they were to be direct. As in France in 1848, in Germany and Finland as well, where semi-presidential systems with a directly elected president were set up (cf. Chapter 2), nothing was borrowed directly from the American model. Once again, what was needed was a functional equivalent for the overthrown monarchy and that was why it was also necessary to take a look at the American model. On the whole, this quickly paled but, on the other hand, relationships with America were less emotionally charged, for instance during the Weimar period – with the exception of the extreme Left and Right. Because of its own isolationism, America had little influence. Ernst Fraenkel gave a very apposite description of the situation:

> In Germany in those days there were pro and anti-Russian tendencies . . . there were anti-English 'continental politicians' and pro-English anti-Bolshevists; there were pan-Europeans and Francophobes. Attitudes towards the USA, on the other hand, had no polarizing effect.[53]

The hour for the American model really seemed to have come after the Second World War. Ultrademocratic constitutions, such as that of the Weimar Republic and the Second Spanish Republic, had failed, *inter alia*, because they had had too few inbuilt checks and balances against

24

concentrations of power. Did not American democracy appear to represent a secure model for the future? In their own sphere of influence, the Soviets imposed their model without hesitation. In Bulgaria and Rumania that simply meant replacing one dictatorship with a different one. In Czechoslovakia or the German Democratic Republic, on the other hand, the Soviet system was superimposed on older democratic traditions. Was that not another apparent reason why the Americans would have to force their model on the defeated powers?

In the light of such pressures, it is fair to say that America was incredibly restrained in pushing forward its own model. The Americans forged ahead with the process of clearing war criminals out of the machinery of government and organizing 'reeducation', especially in Germany. Their success was rather limited, and right-wingers despised what they called 'character cleaning'.[54] The Left, however, also voiced criticism and spurned the American model:

> The American Constitution never served as a model for other countries; it was only adopted by a number of nations, because the United States were in a position to impose it. The first case in point is represented by the Philippines (1899) and the most recent ones, occurring in the period after the Second World War, include Japan and the Federal Republic of Germany. It was only in a number of Latin American states that the constitution was adopted voluntarily – but with the result that the process of decay was completed even more quickly than in the United States itself. All that was left from the example copied was the power of the President, which often took on dictatorial forms.[55]

The above quotation does not suffer from its author actually possessing a knowledge of the facts – especially the first part of it. For the rest, the Americans' influence on the process of elaborating new constitutions for the defeated powers is simply compared with America's imperialist policy in the Philippines, even though this case was far from typical and was regarded as an 'episodic lapse'.[56] Given the power America had, there is all the more reason to express surprise that it did not intervene more strongly in favour of its own model in 1945. In Italy, America's influence was minimal; in Japan, the wish to maintain the institution of Emperor was respected, which precluded the imposition of a presidential system. In Germany, the occupying power only intervened in favour of federalism in order to prevent an excessive concentration of power at national level sometime in the future. Important borrowings on the American model in areas such as federalism and judicial review were not mere *diktats* but had local roots – with the exception of Japan.

The Americans did not interfere with the full democratic exercise of the *'pouvoir constituant'* in the defeated countries, i.e. with the draft constitution approved by the people as a whole (a right the French used to such an extent as to vote 'no' on the first round). There can be no doubt that in Japan and West Germany the work on the constitution was rushed through in a race against time and with a lack of transparency. It is hence no wonder that the Omgus surveys in Germany could only find a 60% approval of the work on the Constitution among the population at large.[57] The democratic flaw in the very origin of the two systems did not, however, give rise to any broad measure of rejection of the new order. Measured in terms of the share of the vote cast for the pro-constitutional parties, the consensus in Germany was even greater than it had been for the German Empire or the Weimar Republic.[58]

The Allies' intervention in the constituent process in the three Western zones of Germany was carried out in accordance with written guidelines (the London agreements, the *Aide-memoire* of November 1948 and the Memorandum of March 1949). Intervention here went further than it did in the setting up of the constitutions of the Federal States (*Länder*). Kurt Schumacher and the SPD never tired of criticizing this intervention. The Allies' recommendations had been kept very general, and, on the whole, they tallied with the view of the majority in Germany – (which was not the case in Japan). In both countries there were serious complaints about the rigid timetable. In Germany this was felt necessary in order to establish a *fait accompli* vis-à-vis the Soviets and the Soviet Occupied Zone. In Japan MacArthur was able to mobilize secret collusion between the occupying power and the government in favour of his own unique form of patronage of the government, by preparing a counterproposal in the Allied Headquarters, once Matsumoto's government's initial draft had been rejected. Although the Japanese government was critical of the Allies' draft, they accepted the principles, most of which appeared alien and sinister to them (in exchange for a handful of concessions from MacArthur, for instance, over the question of a second parliamentary chamber), because they were afraid of the intervention of International Supervisory Councils. The unseemly haste and the numerous concessions were made palatable to the Japanese by the fear that the Far East Commission, which also included the Soviet Union, could insist on a republican constitution and could also force even more extreme concessions. The maintenance of the institution of Emperor had, after all, been one of the Japanese conditions for capitulation.[59] Further pressure was brought to bear on the Japanese, when Whitney, MacArthur's closest deputy, threatened, without any authorization from his commander in-chief (as he himself admitted), to put the American draft of a constitution to the people directly in a referendum.[60]

It was possible to find the legend of American imposition supported in the occasional utterances of German politicians. But these were for tactical reasons as, for instance, in the case of Carlo Schmid, who once maintained that there were certain passages in the Basic Law which had been 'foisted on us'.[61] The military governor, Lucius Clay, reported just the opposite of Carlo Schmid. What he said was: 'He had expected a more rigid position from the military governors and hoped that the Parliamentary Council would be able to take action quickly on our comments'.[62]

The American policy for the democratization of the two defeated powers was very different. In Japan, plans for a military government were dropped; Germany, on the other hand, was subjected to a rigid regime of occupation. In Germany, local initiatives were only permitted at the level of constituent states (*Länder*); in Japan, the implementation of the Potsdam decisions was left to the central government. In both countries the process of drafting new constitutions was forced ahead by the Americans so that they would be able to present the Soviets with *faits accomplis*. In Japan, MacArthur was able to outmanoeuvre the Far Eastern Advisory Commission. The Japanese were ready to stomach even institutions they did not like, since many hoped that this constitution would be only a temporary stop-gap measure.[63] It is surprising that the movement to amend it later on focused less on the foreign imports and more on Article 9, in which Japan renounced armed forces – an article which cannot be ascribed to MacArthur but which came from a Japanese politician. The one institution which seemed to represent the biggest foreign body in Japanese tradition, that of a constitutional court, was assimilated surprisingly well.[64]

In Japan, MacArthur was able to have things all his own way, whereas in Germany it was possible for politicians to play the military governors off against one another in favour of their own ideas. Robertson was ready to leave the Basic Law more or less entirely in the hands of the Germans; the French military governor, König, and Clay, on the other hand, complained at the degree of centralism in the German draft. There were rumours to the effect that the British Labour Party had promised the SPD support for its rigid attitude. The allied intervention was a total success in Japan; in Germany it was a complete failure. One Germano-American political analyst came to the conclusion that:

> In the meantime, the German politicians of 1949 seemed to have learnt more from the debacle of Weimar than the western occupying forces, particularly France. With downright opportunist ingenuity and a form of pragmatism that were completely new to German politics, they were able to ward off the interventions of the occupying authorities with the same skill as that also used, for instance, by groupings which were by inclination more federalist.[65]

American experts on Japan, however, saw the political victory in that country as a Pyrrhic one. What resulted was a 'curious amalgam' of the British and American models. The unicameral parliament and the cabinet system must be seen as 'British', since the Crown was to be retained as a symbolic power. The legal system, on the other hand, was designed on an 'American' basis. It was a 'textbook constitution' drawn up by well-meaning but unprepared civil servants working under enormous pressure of time. Such a constituent process was hardly a good example for learning to apply democratic rules in practice:

> By imposing on the Japanese a constitution hopelessly unsuited to the political ideals or experience of the vast majority of the population, the long term interests of democracy may have been ill served. Instead of a system of government based upon and geared to the social, economic and political realities of the Japanese society, a hollow but elaborate façade modelled after an idealized version of Anglo-American political institutions was hastily patched together. The result is an enormous gap between political fact and constitutional fiction.[66]

Despite such fears, the Japanese system remained surprisingly stable.

Beginning in 1943, Italy managed to evolve from a war enemy of America's to become a sort of 'honorary victor'. There was thus virtually no cause for American involvement in the constituent process. In 1944, the Allied Control Commission had prevented decisions by a Committee of National Liberation (CLN), a conglomeration of all anti-Fascist parties opposed to Badaglio's putsch cabinet, from being implemented. Shortly after the liberation of Rome, in June 1944, however, they abandoned their resistance and, against their better judgement, agreed that the CLN president be called on to head the government.[67] The work of the constituent assembly was completed without Allied intervention. The intellectual influences on the constitution were limited to a few advocates of the presidential system (cf. Chapter 2) and the adoption of constitutional jurisdiction, which had no roots in the Italian legal system (cf. Chapter 4).[68] In none of the other liberated countries did the Americans force their model (not even in Austria). It is especially when viewed in the light of the emerging rivalry with the 'Soviet' model, that the Americans showed themselves, on the whole, to be the most liberal victors of modern times. In no single country was the American model adopted *en bloc*. The process of adoption was limited to individual institutions.

In the most recent wave of redemocratization in Europe, in the southern part of the continent in the 1970s, the American model of democracy played no part. The new parliamentary democracies accepted many different influences and established deliberate ties with national constitutional traditions, such as in Greece in 1974.[69] In Portugal, what emerged was a semi-presidential system with elements of 'socialist pluralism', for which America could not be an example.[70] In

Spain, more time was allowed than anywhere else to study examples in other countries and surprisingly academic debates were conducted during the elaboration of the constitution.[71] The old alternative of choosing between Great Britain and France was balanced out with elements borrowed from many more different sources. Even the Federal Republic of Germany was used as an example for certain institutions (for instance, the constructive vote of no confidence) and the European models in Germany, Italy and Austria had a more direct influence than did the original American model even in the area of constitutional jurisdiction.

Notes

1   Richard Price: *Observations on the Nature of Civil Liberty, the Principles of Government, and the Justice and Policy of the War with America*, London, 1776 (Scholar's Reprints, Dalmar, New York, 1976) p. 98.

2   Marx Engels *Werke*, Berlin (East), Dietz, 1966, Vol. 34, p. 374.

3   Erwin Hölzle: *Russland und Amerika. Aufbruch und Begegnung zweier Weltmächte*, Reinbek, Rowohlt, 1961, pp. 19ff.; Dieter Groh: *Russland und das Selbstverständnis Europas*, Neuwied, Luchterhand, 1961, pp. 138ff.

4   Oswald Spengler: *Jahre der Entscheidung*, Munich, Beck, 1953, p. 52; Hermann Graf Keyserling: *Amerika – der Aufgang einer neuen Welt*, Stuttgart, DVA, 1930, pp. 78ff.

5   Sidney & Beatrice Webb: *The Truth About Soviet Russia*, London, Longmans Green & Co, 1942, p. 16.

6   *Works of John Adams* (Charles Francis Adams, ed.); Boston, 1851, Vol. V, p. 294.

7   Bernard Fay: *L'esprit révolutionnaire en France et aux Etats-Unis à la fin du XVIIIe siècle*, Paris 1924, p. 102; Otto Vossler: *Die amerikanischen Revolutionsideale in ihrem Verhältnis zu den europäischen, untersucht an Thomas Jefferson*, Munich, Oldenbourg, 1929, p. 53.

8   Francis J. Grund: *Aristocracy in America. From the Sketchbook of a German Nobleman*, (London, 1839), Reprint, Gloucester/Mass, Peter Smith, 1968, p. 244.

9   Miss Martineau: *De la société américaine*, Brussels, 1838, p. 11; Max Berger: *The British Traveller in America, 1836-1860*. Gloucester/Mass., Peter Smith, 1964, p. 94.

10   René Rémond: *Les Etats-Unis devant l'opinion française, 1815-1852*, Paris, Colin, 1962, Vol. 2, pp. 660 f.; Donald C. McKay: *The United States and France*, Cambridge/Mass, Harvard UP. 1951. p. 80. On what follows: Charles D. Hazen: *Contemporary American Opinion of the French Revolution*, Baltimore, John Hopkins Press, 1897, pp. 282ff.

11   Friedrich Schlegel: *Philosophie der Geschichte*, in: *Sämtliche Werke*, Vienna 1846, Vol. 14, p. 226.

12   Joseph Priestley: *Letters to the R.H. Edmund Burke* (1791), reprinted in: *The Theological and Miscellaneous Works of Joseph Priestley*, New York (Kraus Reprint) Vol. 22, p. 147.

13   Friedrich von Gentz: Der Ursprung und die Grundsätze der Amerikanischen Revolution, verglichen mit dem Ursprunge und den Grundsätzen der Französischen, in: Historisches Journal, 2 Vol. June 1800, Berlin (101-128), abridged in: Ernst Fraenkel: *Amerika im Spiegel des deutschen politischen Denkens*, Cologne/ Opladen, Westdeutscher Verlag, 1959, pp. 79-81.

14   Some references in: Reinhard Koselleck, *Revolution*, in: Otto Brunner et al. (ed.): *Geschichtliche Grundbegriffe. Historisches Lexikon zur politisch-sozialen Sprache in Deutschland*, Stuttgart, Klett-Cotta, 1984, Vol. 5 (653-788), p. 724.

15   *Revolution*, in: Rotteck/Welcker: *Staatslexikon*, Altona, Hammerich, 1841, Vol. 13 (722-740) p. 724.

16   Herbert P. Gallinger: *Die Haltung der deutschen Publizistik zu dem Amerikanischen Unabhängigkeitskriege*, 1775-1783, thesis. Leipzig, 1900, p. 77; Thomas K. Gorman: *America and Belgium. A Study of the Influence of the United States upon the Belgian Revolution of 1789-1790*, London, F. Fisher Unwin, 1925, p. 269.

17   George G. Bancroft: *History of the United States*, Boston, 1879, Vol. 3, pp. 10ff; Clinton Rossiter: *Seedtime of the Republic*, New York, 1953, pp. 352ff.

18   R.R. Palmer: *The Age of the Democratic Revolution*, Princeton UP, 1959, Vol. 1, p. 188. Karl-Heinz Röder: *Das politische System der USA. Geschichte und Gegenwart*, Berlin (East), Staatsverlag der DDR, 1980, p. 32.

19   Hannah Arendt: *On Revolution*, New York, Harcourt & Brace, 1963, Chapter 3; Dolf Sternberger: *Drei Wurzeln der Politik*. Frankfurt, Insel, 1978, p. 403; Ghita Ionescu: *Politics and the Pursuit of Happiness*, London, Longman, 1984, p. 28. On the Jefferson swindle from the psychological viewpoint – Paul Watzlawick: *Gebrauchsanweisung für Amerika*, Munich, Piper, 1984, 8th Edn., p. 136.

20   Alexis de Tocqueville: *De la démocratie en Amérique*, Paris (*Oeuvres complètes*, Vol. 1), Gallimard, 1961, p. 14.

21   Karl Salomo Zachariae: *Vierzig Bücher vom Staate*, Heidelberg, Winter, 1839, Theil 3, pp. 219ff.

22   Murhard: *Nordamerikanische Verfassung*, in: Rotteck/Welcker: *Staats-Lexikon*, op. cit. Vol. 11 (381-465), p. 412.

23   L.L. Matthias: *Die Kehrseite der USA*, Reinbek, Rowohlt, 1964, pp. 21ff.

24   Ralph Barton Perry: *Puritanism and Democracy*, New York, 1944, Chapter 8.6.

25   Ernst Fraenkel: *Das amerikanische Regierungssystem*, Cologne, Westdeutscher Verlag, 1962, p. 37.

26   Heinrich von Treitschke: *Politik*, Leipzig. Hirzel, 1898, Vol. 2, p. 272.

27   Manfred Hennigsen: *Der Fall Amerika. Zur Sozial- und Bewusstseinsgeschichte einer Verdrängung. Das Amerika der Europäer*, Munich, List, 1974, pp. 76ff.

28   Carl J. Friedrich: *The Impact of American Constitutionalism Abroad*, Boston UP, 1967, p. 4.

29   Rémond, op. cit. pp. 660ff, 720; Zachariae. op. cit. p. 215.

30   J.J. Rüttimann: *Das nordamerikanische Bundesstaatsrecht, verglichen mit den politischen Einrichtungen der Schweiz*, Zurich, Orell & Füssli, 1867, Part 1, p. 16.

31   Eugene Newton Curtis: *The French Assembly of 1848 and the American Constitutional Doctrines*, New York, Columbia University, PhD thesis, 1917, p. 146.

32   Chateaubriand: *Mémoires d'outre-tombe*, Paris, Flammarion, Vol. 1, 1982 (Book 8, Ch. 11), 1982, p. 351; G.W.F. Hegel: *Die Vernunft in der Geschichte*, Hamburg, Meiner, ed. J. Hoffmeister, 1955, 5th Edition, p. 207;

33   Franz Wigard (ed.): *Stenographischer Bericht über die Verhandlungen der deutschen constituirenden Nationalversammlung zu Frankfurt am Main*. 1848, Vol. 5, p. 3616, col. 1.

34   Rémond, op. cit., p. 833; Curtis, op. cit., pp. 69ff.

35   Curtis, op. cit., p. 79.

36   Andrew J. Torrielli: *Italian Opinion on America as revealed by Italian Travellers, 1850-1900*, Cambridge/Mass, Harvard UP, 1941 (New York, Kraus Reprint, 1969, p. 48).

37   Curtis, op. cit., p. 147.

38 Klaus von Beyme: *Karl Marx and Party Theory. Government and Opposition*, 1985, pp. 70-87.
39 *MEW*, Vol. 27, p. 570; Alexander Trachtenberg (ed.): *Letters to Americans. 1848-1895*, New York, 1953, pp. 25ff.
40 Robert Laurence Moore: *European Socialists and the American Promised Land*, New York, Oxford UP, 1970, p. 5.
41 *MEW*, Vol. 28, p. 507; Trachtenberg, op. cit., pp. 44f.
42 *MEW*, Vol. 18, p. 160.
43 *MEW*, Vol. 35, p. 200 (Letter to Sorge 20.6.1881).
44 *MEW*, Vol. 36, p. 505 (Letter to Kelley-Wischnewetzky 13.8.1886).
45 *MEW*, Vol. 36, p. 533.
46 *MEW*, Vol. 36, p. 689, Vol. 38, p. 313; Trachtenberg, op. cit., pp. 242ff.
47 *MEW*, Vol. 39, p. 249 (to Sorge, 12th May, 1894); Trachtenberg, op. cit., p. 263.
48 Werner Somnbart: *Warum gibt es in den Vereinigten Staaten keinen Sozialismus?* Tübingen, Mohr, 1906.
49 Theodore J. Lowi: Why is There no Socialism in the United States? A Federal Analysis. *International Political Science Review*, 1984, pp. 369-380.
50 Fraenkel, op. cit., p. 41.
51 V. I. Lenin: *Die nächsten Aufgaben der Sowjetmacht.* In: Ausgewählte Werke, Berlin (East), Dietz, 1966, Vol. 2, p. 753.
52 Eduard His: *Amerikanische Einflüsse im Schweizerischen Verfassungsrecht*, In: *Festgabe der Basler Juristenfakultät und des Basler Juristenvereins zum Schweizerischen Juristentag*, Basle, Helbing & Lichtenhahn, 1920 (81-110), p. 110; Myron Luehrs Tripp: *Der schweizerische und der amerikanische Bundesstaat*, Zurich, Polygraphischer Verlag, 1942, p. 58.
53 Fraenkel, op. cit., p. 44.
54 Caspar Schrenck-Notzing: *Charackterwäsche*, Stuttgart, Seewald, 1965, esp. p. 221.
55 Matthias, op. cit., (Note 23), p. 21; On criticism of left-wing anti-Americanism: Hartmut Wasser: *Die USA – der unbekannte Partner*, Paderborn, Schöningh, 1983, pp. 33ff.
56 Knud Krakau: *Missionsbewusstsein und Völkerrechtsdoktrin in den Vereinigten Staaten von Amerika*, Frankfurt, Metzner, 1967, p. 176.
57 Anna J. Merritt/Richard L. Merritt (ed.): *Public Opinion in Occupied Germany. The OMGUS Surveys 1945-1949*, Urbana University of Illinois Press, 1970, p. 307.
58 For Japan: John M. Maki: *Government and Politics in Japan. The Road to Democracy*, New York, Praeger, 1962, p. 77.
59 Hans H. Baerwald: *Japan's Parliament*, Cambridge UP, 1974, p. 9.
60 Courtney Whitney: *MacArthur, His Rendezvous with History*, New York, Knopf, 1956, pp. 251ff.; T. Ohgushi: *Die japanische Verfassung vom 3. November 1946. Jahrbuch des Öffentlichen Rechts*, Tübingen, Mohr, 1956, p. 302; Theodore H. McNelly: *Domestic and International Influences on Constitutional Revision in Japan 1945-1946*, New York, Columbia UP, PhD thesis, 1952.
61 *Documents on the Creation of the German Federal Constitution. US Military Government, Civil Administration Department*, Berlin, 1949, p. 78.
62 Lucius D. Clay: *Decision in Germany*, Garden City, Doubleday, 1950, p. 422.
63 Kaoru Matsumoto: *The question of constitutional revision in Japan*, in: Karl Dietrich Bracher et al. (eds): *Die moderne Demokratie und ihr Recht. Festschrift für Gerhard Leibholz zum 65. Geburtstag*, Tübingen, Mohr, 1966, Vol. 2 (851-876), p. 852.
64 Kazahiro Hayashida: *Constitutional Court and Supreme Court of Japan*, ibid. Vol. 2 (407-426), p. 421.

65   Peter H. Merkl: *Die Entstehung der Bundesrepublik Deutschland*, Stuttgart, Kohlhammer, 1969, 2nd edn., p. 141; *The Origin of the West German Republic*, New York, Oxford UP, 1953.
66   Robert E. Ward: The Origins of the Present Japanese Constitution, *APSR*, 1956 (980-1110), p. 1010.
67   Piero Calamandrei: *Costruire la democrazia. Premesse alla costituente*, Florence, no date (1945), pp. 35ff.
68   cf Roberto Ruffili: *Cultura politica e partiti nell' età della costituente*, Bologna, Il Mulino, 1979, 2 Vols.
69   Ioannis Kassaras: *Die griechische Verfassung von 1975*, Heidelberg, v. Decker/ Schenck, 1983, p. 12.
70   Rainer Eisfeld: *Sozialistischer Pluralismus in Europa. Ansätze und Scheitern am Beispiel Portugal*, Cologne, Verlag Wissenschaft und Politik, 1984, pp. 152ff.
71   Luis Sánchez-Agesta: *Sistema político de la constitución española de 1978*, Madrid, Editora Nacional, 1980, p. 60.

2   The Presidential System of Government

Origin of the term 'Presidential System of Government'

It was only relatively late that constitutional scholars began to consider the presidential system of government as a form of rule in its own right. As long as the classical definition system for types of government continued to predominate, the American system was seen as a variation of the republic and not classified in any more detail in terms of the relationship between the powers. It was only when the need was felt to make subdivisions within the then commonest form of government, constitutional monarchy, in order to be able to distinguish different systems, such as Great Britain, the July Monarchy or Prussia, that more attention was also focused on classifying the republics. The question of the origin of the head of state, which was the basis of the subdivision between republics and monarchies, became less important than the question of the relationship between the most important powers within a system. It was only about half way through the nineteenth century that the idea of a separate classification for the representative constitutions as a function of their strongest or most distinctive institution won the day. The emergence of the term 'parliamentary government' pioneered this development. It was still occasionally maintained that the term 'presidential system of government' was misleading, since Congress and President had been conceived of as equal and independent institutions which had waged a battle for supremacy with varying degrees of success right into the twentieth century. In his classification

33

of 'thirteen forms of rule', Carl Joachim Friedrich accommodated this dualism by using the term 'presidential-congressional system of government'.[1] A number of observers have expressed irritation at the large number of terms used to define the American system. For a long time, the term 'presidential government' was maintained along with the thesis that there was actually 'congressional government'.

The term 'presidential system' could not come into being as long as it was felt that Congress was the strongest institution within the system. Even Tocqueville (who had expressed concern in his analysis of the strengthening of the office of President under Jackson) was still maintaining that *le pouvoir prépondérant réside dans la réprésentation nationale toute entière* ('the dominant power is in the hands of national representation in its entirety').[2] From this point of view, the term 'congressional government', which was subsequently used in a polemical fashion, would in no way have appeared discriminating. To push the comparison to extremes, it could be said that whereas it had become questionable to apply the expression 'parliamentary government' as early as the second English Parliamentary Reform of 1867, and that when it was most widely used the British system had actually once again grown out of being 'parliamentary government' in the literal sense, it could also be argued that the 'presidential system' has only come to satisfy the full meaning of the term during the twentieth century. It was only in this century that the president (with few interruptions) became the strongest power within the system.

Among non-American writers who used the term 'presidential system' were Bagehot and Mohl. In his *Encyclopaedia of Government Sciences* Mohl contrasted 'presidential government' with 'government by directory' and 'government by assembly'.[3] In his 1860 essay on 'the appointment of the executive power in the representative democracies', Mohl made one further distinction. He subdivided systems where the assembly itself maintained executive power (government by assembly), Swiss-type government by directory, and systems where the Executive was placed in the hands of one individual. In those days, there was still no short name for such systems and hence he subsumed within this third group both the American Constitution and that of the Second French Republic (which was not strictly correct),[4] even though, in an appreciative comment on the 1848 French Constitution, he had clearly stressed the semiparliamentary character of that system. In an essay on 'The Further Development of the Democratic Principle in North American Constitutional Law', Mohl once again only used the generic term 'representative democracy'.[5] Presumably, the acceptance of the term 'presidential system of government' by Mohl (the leading authority on comparative political writing of his time) can be taken as typical for terminological developments. Whereas the term 'parliamentary government' was more widely used in the 1830s and 1840s, the term 'presidential system' only became established in the late 1860s.

An attempt was made to group together the 'dualist systems' as a single form of government, whereby the 'presidential system' appeared to be a close relation of constitutional monarchy, government by directory and the Latin American form of the President in the Council of Ministers.[6] In terms of the genesis of the two systems, there is doubtless justification for underlining the close relationship between constitutional monarchy and the presidential system of government, but this does run the risk of concealing the functional difference to the present-day American system. Its party structure and modern techniques of government have made it more like the non-dualist parliamentary system than nineteenth-century constitutional monarchy in several respects.[7] The inclusion of the special form 'President in Council of Ministers' among the dualist systems also has its problems. Between the dualist and the parliamentary systems there is a whole range of semipresidential or semiparliamentary systems with quite different separations of powers. The term *'Präsidialregierung'* ('presidial government') so beloved in Germany to describe the Weimar system, in which the direct election of the President was the only feature in common with the true presidential system, has often had a misleading effect and concealed the underlying parliamentary nature of that constitution. The Second French Republic, a number of South American constitutions and the Fifth Republic by no means clearly belong to the dualist systems; they are rather hybrid forms, which (depending on the way they operate in practice) defy virtually any classification within traditional patterns.

Criticisms of the presidential system among American writers and reactions to these in Europe

Advocates of the presidential system in Europe had an uphill struggle in constitutional assemblies and in the press, since their opponents were able to make use of extensive heated arguments levelled by Americans against their own system. The attempts of dissatisfied individuals to overcome the dualism in the system are as old as the Constitution itself.

It has often been said that the American Constitution was a pretty realistic republican copy of the English one in accordance with eighteenth-century constitutional doctrine and that the American Constitution maintained the features of the older (preparliamentary) British Constitution in a purer form than in Great Britain itself. However, that must not be allowed to conceal the fact that many of the fathers of the Constitution gathered at the Philadelphia Convention rejected the

English example in its entirety, since they did not believe that a 'republican' imitation of England's monarchist constitution was possible. Wilson of Pennsylvania, who had actually been born in Scotland, was one of their most vociferous spokesmen and it is no coincidence that he advocated a strong, undivided executive close to the people.[8] The outcome of the Convention was by no means a foregone conclusion. There had been advocates of other systems which were more similar to later continental parliamentary systems than to the American solution. Roger Sherman from Connecticut had put forward the point of view that the incumbent of the executive 'ought to be appointed by and accountable to the Legislature only'.[9] Wilson, on the other hand, saw the executive's dependence on the legislature as the 'very essence of tyranny'.[10] In the eyes of later doctrinaire conservatives of 'genuine parliamentarism', Sherman would have counted as a supporter of government by assembly. The separation of powers within the presidential system turned out to be a compromise between competing constitutional ideas.

By no means did this compromise create a dualism of fully equal powers, as many subsequent eulogists of the American constitution with its separation of powers, seemed to assume. The executive, from which the name of the present-day system is derived, was subject to many different checks. The indirect system of election was designed to mitigate the components of plebiscitary democracy in the appointment of the president. It is only since Jackson's time that the system for electing the president has developed more in a plebiscitary direction. To begin with, the interpreters of the American constitution agreed that it was the legislature that had the higher rank. A sentence from *Federalist 51* is often quoted: 'In republican government, the legislative authority necessarily predominates'.[11] What is much less frequently quoted, on the other hand, is the continuation of the same sentence, in which the author (Hamilton or Madison) implicitly admitted that this could lead to difficulties for the government. He saw the division of the legislature as a guarantee against congressional despotism but did not rule out that 'the weakness of the Executive may require, on the other hand, that it should be fortified'.[12]

Hamilton had already had painful practical government experience of the gulf between the cabinet and Congress. He was one of the first to try, as the holder of a government office, to exert stronger influence over Congress. In Burns' writings, Hamilton is actually seen as the intellectual father of the interpretation of the American constitution in the sense of 'presidential government'.[13] All the hopes of those individuals who wanted to develop the American system along similar lines to those parliamentary systems with close ties between the two most important powers, were in vain. Despite the supremacy of the legislature, the American system had no means of developing into a parliamentary system without radical amendments to the constitution.

During the American Civil War, the two sides took on opposing constitutional paths. Lincoln was successful in strengthening the office of President decisively for the duration of the war. After his death, the consequence of this was a setback which culminated in the impeachment attempt against President Johnson. On the other hand, Jefferson Davis, at the head of the government of the Confederate States in the South, was, for period of time, virtually reduced to the level of a president in the parliamentary system, despite the fact that the structure of the Constitution and that of the founding fathers were as alike as two peas in a pod. Stephens went so far as to campaign for a rule obliging the president of the Confederate States to recruit his cabinet from among members of the Congress.[14] In May 1861, John Perkins suggested that at least members of the cabinet should be allowed to speak in the House, which was approved by four states and rejected by two, with one state splitting its vote. In 1863 it was decided to bring the duration of the cabinet's period in office into line with that of the legislature. The intention was to force President Davis to reappoint his cabinet every two years. Early in 1865 the conflict between president and Congress reached a climax. The Virginia Delegation demanded the resignation of the whole cabinet, whereupon War Secretary James A. Seddon, himself from Virginia, promptly resigned.[15] It is not impossible that the confederate system would have moved nearer to a parliamentary one had it been allowed to exist for a long period of time. At all events, it is fair to think that it would have developed into a semidualist presidential system along the lines of the Second French Republic.

Throughout the long period of weakness of the presidency in the aftermath of the Civil War, a broad-ranging controversy arose over the dominant position of Congress. Only on rare occasions, however, were calls made for more parliamentarism in the American system, as in some of the essays written by Woodrow Wilson, later to become president. But Wilson was not consistent in his propaganda in favour of cabinet government on the English pattern, although his own clumsiness in his dealings with Congress as president seemed to prove his thesis right after the event. The arguments against congressional government, which Wilson popularized in his book of the same name, basically had a much more limited objective, however much Wilson may have criticized the unclear responsibility in the presidential system, of which he said that 'it parcels out power and confuses responsibility'.[16]

Thomas K. Finletter, William Yandell Elliot, Walter Lippmann or David Lawrence,[17] who were at times accused of wanting to abolish the presidential system and replace it with a parliamentary one, were either usually only thinking in terms of modifications to the presidential system or subsequently moved away from proposals for more parliamentarism and opted for less far-reaching alternatives. Walter Lippmann, for example, had not wanted to make the executive generally dependent on congressional votes but merely proposed that secretaries of state should resign after mid-term elections if it was felt that they could be made responsible for losses in such elections. This proposal had the drawback that it was hardly possible to ascertain with any degree of precision whose area of competence had prompted the greatest criticism. For technical reasons, it happens now and again that the fiercest criticism in an electoral campaign is not directed against the worst secretary of state. At all events, the resignation of a secretary of state for such reasons would inevitably do further damage to the standing of the president who had appointed him, in addition to the electoral defeat.

The Americans' criticism of their own system has been repeatedly used to polarize the conflict between the presidential and the parliamentary system, and this built up very effective counter-propaganda against the adoption of the presidential constitution in Europe. The arguments of those favouring this system were greatly weakened by the fact that it could be pointed out that a large number of political writers in America were not happy with the system that was being recommended to other countries.

Even Pendleton's early endeavours to reform the Constitution were used as arguments in the first written attempts to analyse the possibility of adopting the presidential system in European states. In his remarkable book researching dissatisfaction with the presidential system and published in 1886, the Italian, Livio Minguzzi, expressly went as far back as Roger Sherman and Pendleton.[18] He was, however, quite right in his forecast that the majority of Americans would always offer resistance to attempts to move their presidential system towards a parliamentary one. One of the last wrangles between Americans and Europeans regarding the quality of the two comparative systems to be given major prominence in the press was that between Price and Laski in 1943–44. Price expressed his concern that only psychoanalysts could explain the secret longing of so many Americans for the institutions of their 'mother land', England.[19] The criticism which Laski had to make of the presidential system added a number of further arguments to the complaints dealt with above regarding the lack of adequate presidential leadership and the tendency for the presidential system to degenerate into 'congressional government'. His arguments are so typical of those mustered against the American system that they are given here *pars pro toto*:

1   Price made reference to changes in the American system of administration, but Laski stuck to his rejection of the American spoil

system. As a representative of the Left, Laski stuck with tremendous resilience to the prejudices of conservative critics of America from Tocqueville right through to Max Weber. Until well into the twentieth century, it was regarded as axiomatic that the spoil system was a consequence of constitutional dualism. We find Hugo Preuss, for instance, making the following assertion:

> The parliamentary system takes the political leadership, which does not suit the nature of a professional civil service, away from it and causes it to undergo certain changes; apart from that, the two are not only compatible with each other but complement one another in a perfectly felicitous fashion. The spoil system as a consequence of dualism was something that a professional civil service must surely destroy.[20]

In making such claims, the defenders of the parliamentary system forgot that it was precisely that system with its tendency to party government which for a long time had been subject to the accusation from advocates of constitutional monarchy in Europe that it replaced the recruitment of technically competent civil servants and ministers with sharing out the spoils to the party faithful. The particular roots of the spoil system and the reasons the civil service developed late in America were only rarely analysed. On the other hand, the fact that England was also late in developing its civil service was viewed as very definitely positive by the eulogists of British self-government. This criticism does not, of course, set out to deny the fact that the development of ministerial accountability before parliament within the parliamentary system has influenced the formation of the professional civil service in several countries. This particular link is one which the critics of the presidential system have belaboured far too much, connecting it with the inadmissible reverse conclusion that it is the dualist presidential system which is primarily responsible for the absence of a professional civil service in America. With the continuing development of the modern presidential system, it is an argument that is, however, rapidly losing ground.

2   The presidential system was also accused of giving excessive authority to the third power, the 'Supreme Court', which Laski actually dubbed 'the Third Chamber' and which, he believed, made use of judicial review to exercise political patronage over the people as a whole, thereby seriously impeding social change in accordance with the will of the majority. The inability of American Presidents to cope with the racial problem constantly refuelled this argument right into the Johnson era. However, it has become increasingly generally recognized that today parts of so-called majority opinion represent a much bigger barrier to solving the civil rights issues than does the Supreme Court. In

addition, there are grounds for doubting that the conservative function of the Supreme Court in American history can really be ascribed solely to the presidential system. Once again, in the absence of true comparisons, it is popular to depict the Supreme Court in its American form as a necessary functional element of the presidential system (cf. Chapter IV).

3   Whereas American research into interest groups rightly emphasizes their integrating effect inside the dualist system, Laski maintained that, through its separation of powers, the presidential system created greater opportunities for pressure groups and ones which were much more difficult to keep under control than in the parliamentary system with its clear-cut responsibilities.[21] Some of the causes of this, on which Laski placed heavy emphasis, are not necessarily linked to the dualist construction of the constitution but are connected with the residence requirement, the dominance of local notabilities, and federalism. It may well be that the congressman, of whom the story is told that he sweated it out through the mid-summer heat in Washington because he dared not return home on vacation until such time as he was able to secure some promised concession for a powerful man in his constituency, such as the owner of a department store, is typical of America. It is very difficult to make the presidential system *per se* responsible for such abuses.

The Campaign for the presidential system of government in Europe

Experience has shown that campaigns for a constitution following the American pattern were linked to particular social conditions, which recurred in the various countries.

1   The break in monarchist legitimacy created a certain constitutional and ideological vacuum which helped propaganda in favour of the presidential system. It was only where there was a genuine chance of introducing a republican constitution that the American example could exert a strong influence.

The European monarchies, all of which, without exception, continued to develop into parliamentary monarchies, were not a favourable terrain for propagating the American system. In monarchies where parliaments had developed, however, the call for a return to the dualist-type constitution had the same function as the call for the presidential system among republicans. Italy, Belgium and Sweden have all gone through phases where large parts of the political press have advocated the move away from parliamentary monarchy again. It was in *Italy* that this campaign took on the biggest proportions. It became known by the slogan which the subsequent conservative head of the government, Sidney Sonnino, popularized by means of a newspaper article in 1897: 'Torniamo allo statuto' ('Back to the Statute!').[22] Sonnino and many other discontented individuals demanded a return to the dualist constitutional system of the 1848 Statute with only minor concessions to the parliamentary system which had developed in the meantime under that constitution. In the process, the discussion on the presidential system of government was a purely academic one, except where the critics were republicans wanting to abolish the Italian monarchy. It did, however, happen that the advantages of the presidential system were occasionally outlined; they were, nonetheless, only used as a comparison to explain the advantages which a 'reconstitutionaliza-tion' of the system could also offer.[23] On the other hand, the proponents of the parliamentary system tried to use the presidential system to bring out the disadvantages of the dualist constitution, in the hope of showing the opportunities of the parliamentary system in better light.[24]

In Spain, the greatest statesman of the restored monarchy, Cánovas de Castillo, had nothing but admiration for many aspects of the presidential system and defended it against the virulent criticisms voiced by James Bryce of England.[25] It was Cánovas' hope that with a semiparliamentary, semiconstitutional monarchy (with ministers having dual responsibility to Parliament and the Monarch) he would be able to achieve the stability of government for which he so envied America. In Belgium, the much-travelled expert on foreign systems of government, Émile de Laveleye, was very positive in explaining the advantages of the presidential system over the parliamentary one. He found particular words of praise for the fact that the American President was able to choose his ministers according to objective criteria and the Secretaries of State did not constantly need to have one eye on the majority.[26]

The American model could only have concrete effects in the second period of its adoption, after 1948, when republican constitutions were being created in Europe. American influence was at its strongest in setting up the *Second French Republic*, even if it is an exaggeration to say that this was the only attempt ever to transplant the American Constitution to Europe.[27]

Convinced Radical Republicans have only rarely used the presidential system as their model. They were, anyway, more inclined towards the constitutions of the French Revolution, and amongst their most important constitutional political examples they counted government by convention, the Directory constitution and the consular republic. It was the Gironde Constitution which had the greatest influence on the 1948 Republicans. The chairman of the constitutional committee of the Constituent Assembly of 1848, Cormenin, did not even mention the American solution in his introduction to possibilities for setting up a republican executive. He outlined three alternatives:

1   The Assembly would exercise the powers of the Executive itself through delegates (government by convention)

2   The appointment of three or five Consuls or Directors

3   The election of a President or of Consuls.

To begin with, Cormenin was not thinking of a directly elected president or even a president elected by indirect universal suffrage in accordance with the American example.[28] The committee decided in favour of a president virtually without debate; it was only the question as to whether he should be elected by parliament or by the people as a whole that led to lengthy wrangling. The proposal made by Dupin, a one-time Orleanist, to give the head of the Executive the title '*Président de la République*' was accepted. The extent to which the American example was a key factor in his preference for such a title is something it is difficult to decide. Once the decision in favour of a president had been taken, the chairman of the constitutional committee, Cormenin, then decided that he, too would try to go along with that development and advocated that the president be elected directly. It seems that the creation of the office of President in the Second Republic had been influenced less by the American example and more by the need to reach a compromise between Republicans and Orleanists. Typical of the opportunist Republicans, who allowed themselves to be guided by the Orleanist example, were Odilon Barrot, Duvergier de Hauranne and Tocqueville, who accepted the semipresidential constitution in order to prevent the ultra-parliamentarian government by convention, which the convinced Republicans would presumably have introduced had they had a free hand. In the constitutional committee, Tocqueville and his friend, Beaumont, demanded presidential prerogatives '*à peu près d'un roi constitutionnel*' (more or less those of a constitutional monarch) – quite apart from the period in office, immunity and unaccountability.[29]

In the National Assembly, the committee's draft was criticized by many for borrowing too many aspects from the American system. Deputy Parieu repeated the argument that had been heard frequently that America's system was incapable of being transferred. It could only function where there were no monarchists, where no unitary state was possible, and where there was no need to be excessively mistrustful in setting up the constitution, since there had never been any doubt that the first President of the United States would be a man of integrity.[30]

42

The example of America was used to criticize the position of the proposed President, who would not even have the right of veto of a constitutional monarch vis-à-vis the Assembly. Parieu summed up his criticism of the draft in one sentence: the President had been given the roots of an oak but the head of a rose. Several of the reluctant Republicans did, however, defend the semidualist structure. Tocqueville, for instance, fought against the idea of the President being elected by parliament.[31] For him, the choice within the republican form of government was simply between 'government by convention' or 'presidential government'. In those days the parliamentary republic was still equated with the convention system. For reasons of the separation of powers, 'gouvernement républicain' (republican government) meant the same to him as 'pouvoir exécutif électif' (elected executive).[32] All attempts to make the Second Republic's system decisively more 'presidential', which were aimed primarily at abolishing ministerial accountability before Parliament and the compatibility between parliamentary mandate and ministerial office, failed. In 1849 Frédéric Bastiat was still fighting against compatibility and, in impassioned speeches and written articles, he urged the 'representatives of the citizenry' to look towards America: 'Should the ministry be recruited in the Chambers? England says yes and is in a bad way. America says no and it is doing fine.'[33]

In the *German Paulskirche* system there was a rare case of the presidential system being discussed in a federation of monarchies. Investigations into the American influence on the *Paulskirche* Constitution stress that it was probably greater than that of the English or French model.[34] That only applies, however, to attempts to set up a federal state. The many lengthy pro-American articles published in 1848 show no clear grasp of the relationship between President and Congress in America. Bunsen, the Prussian Envoy in London, who was among the few officials representing the German States to approve the draft of the Committee of Seventeen, contrasted the 'American formula' with the 'Anglo-Belgian' (i.e. parliamentary) one. However, he wanted to combine the American solution with constitutional monarchy and he hoped that out of this combination Germany would develop a particular type and would elevate it to 'a higher plane of validity'.[35] Even the plans to set up a Directory of Three Princes, which were frequently decried as semirepublican, would only have permitted a presidential system in isolated points (e.g. incompatibility and the ministers' dependence on the trust of the Directory). It was, however, precisely the unity of the executive, so highly praised in the American system, which it would not have been possible to implement. Republicans and Radicals did not even have a love of federalism to motivate them to speak out in favour of an American system, so Blum, Trützschler and other left-wingers tended to favour an extreme parliamentary form of government by assembly.

The seventeen's constitutional draft itself and the draft of the preliminary commission had certain similarities with the American Constitution. Among the speakers in the *Paulskirche* there were many admirers of the American Constitution but few of them thought in terms of adopting the American solution in its entirety.[36] An amendment tabled on 28th March 1849 by von Diskau, a member of the Assembly, came nearest to the American solution for the Head of the Executive. It read: 'The executive power in the German Empire shall be entrusted to an *accountable* president to be elected by the people for a duration of four years. A Vice-President shall be chosen to assist the President. Any German citizen may stand for election.'[37] However, the Republicans remained in the minority.

It was those in favour of a hereditary emperor who won the day, although individual members tried to prove that there was no major difference between an American-style president and a constitutional monarch with few rights, such as those enjoyed by the 'Norwegian' king (e.g. the right of veto). The Republicans were, however, not to be convinced. The accountability of the American president seemed to them to represent a protection against abuses which they believed they could not do without. The Republican member from Giessen, Vogt, admitted that in countries like England, where a deeply-rooted feeling for freedom was a living matter, certain aspects (such as the English monarch's right of veto) could be tolerated 'on paper'. He went on, however, to add: 'If we had that as well, then I would be ready to let you put any form of words, nay everything you want, down on paper; for I would know that the spirit alive in every individual would break through such a formulation or hold it in check, but, given our circumstances, nothing can be allowed to be put on paper; for we know too well, that it will indeed be used.'[38] The very idea that an unaccountable president, especially if he was also a prince, could use the veto seemed to him intolerable. In the whole process, however, even less thought was spared for the reality of the American president's accountability than the use of the veto by constitutional monarchs in the real political world of the time. Claussen, the member representing Kiel, who was accustomed to saying harsh things about monarchs in general and more specifically about the prince of his own country, Schleswig-Holstein, made the following statement on that particular point: 'I have explained my view as to why the president or the directory must be accountable in the same way the president of North America is; i.e. that he would not be forced to resign if a vote in the National Assembly went against him, instead of which he would appoint new ministers, but accountability would also not mean that, were he to commit high treason, he would be exonerated and enjoy the privilege of immunity before the law.'[39] From these words, it was possible to take it that the ministers would be subject to a two-fold accountability, to parliament and to the president, whereby the intention was that it would only be possible to enforce accountability to parliament indirectly via the president's right to remove them from office. Of itself, this view did not entirely tally with the American system, where, up until the present, it is not expected of the President that he change a Secretary of State who meets with no-confidence in Congress, and where, indeed, the rules of procedure would make no allowance for votes of censure.

Even the most ardent supporters of the American system of an accountable president elected by universal suffrage were not in favour of a one-hundred percent implementation of the presidential system. In the *Paulskirche* they also allowed themselves to go in for the same compromise as that represented by the Second French Republic, in the form of a hybrid solution.

In the same way, federalism and a republican view of the accountability of the head of state and ministers did not produce a clear-cut presidential concept for the future *Paulskirche* Constitution in Germany, it led generally to a semipresidential, hybrid system – as indeed nearly everywhere on the European continent. Where federalism became the central topic of the debates on the constitution, it was not usually the presidential system that won the day either, it was another dualist system, the Swiss Council system, which was more strongly promoted. A good example of this is Australia (cf. Chapter 4).

2   In the second phase of the adoption of the model of American institutions, after the First World War, what was required was even less the integral adoption of the presidential system and much more the creation of a functional equivalent to the monarchy under republican conditions, with concessions being made to the monarchist feelings of a sizable minority. The Weimar Republic and Finland are the most important examples of this.

The Weimar Constituents of 1919 found themselves in a position which in several ways was similar to that of the French in 1848. A revolution had overthrown the monarchy, yet monarchist feelings and the ideal of a dualist-type constitution were still widely held. In Weimar in 1919 there were also 'Republicans despite themselves'; only a few German Nationalists, such as Count Posadowsky-Wehner or von Delbrück, actually engaged publicly in pro-monarchist propaganda. For only a few, however, was the search for a 'substitute *Kaiser*' prompted by a *dolus eventualis* in favour of a restoration of the monarchy. Only a few were naive enough to hope that the election of the president by universal suffrage might some day permit the candidature of a Hohenzollern pretender. The most perceptive among the German Nationalists were also motivated by a genuine concern for a constitutional balance in the republic, and the directly elected president was to be the republican form of the constitutional monarch. That being the objective, no demand for a truly presidential system emerged in the German Nationalist camp. Efforts were made, for instance, to ensure that the president's right to dissolve parliament and the right to order a plebiscite would not require countersignature, but the Nationalists were ready to tolerate the idea of a cabinet between the president and the *Reichstag* – an idea that is just as incompatible with presidential government as were the extensive plans regarding dissolution. The Constitutional Committee's rapporteur, Ablass (DDP), was in favour of Delbrück's proposals but, at the same time, defended the basic parliamentary concept of Preuss's draft and stressed that neither the Committee nor the majority in the National Assembly wanted to adopt either the French or the American system.[40]

The motives which encouraged Hugo Preuss (and, above all, Max Weber) to plead in favour of a *Präsidialsystem* were also connected with the break in continuity and legitimacy. Max Weber recommended going for the American system (at least according to a report by Ritzler, who accompanied Weber when he met Ebert). When Ebert, however, asked him about the spoil system in the United States, Weber certainly did not try to deny the drawbacks of the American system. It is to be assumed that this report has grossly simplified the discussions between Ebert and Weber. In Weber's own writings there are only very few hints that he was in favour of a full presidential system. On the other hand, he was far too knowledgeable to let the spoil system stand as an objection to the American system of the separation of powers, with which it was only very remotely linked, so the best thing to do is to take Weber's written word at face value. All he ever advocated was a system with a president elected by the people to fill the vacuum in legitimation left by the house of Hohenzollern.[41] Weber regarded the dynasties as so compromised that he felt he could dare to mimic the position of a monarch in the form of the plebiscitary head of the republic, without doing anything to advance the cause of restoration. By the same token, he aimed to bring 'Monarchist grist to the Republican-Democratic mill'. The term used by Weber in *Wirtschaft und Gesellschaft* to describe the Weimar solution, 'plebiscitary-representative government', was more correct than the commonly-used expression 'presidential constitution'.

Preuss, who began by preferring the traditional form of appointment by parliament, came round to the idea of electing the president directly (not without being influenced by Max Weber). The fear that the system might degenerate into a form of 'artificial French parliamentarism' led to the idea that it would be possible to combine the advantages of the American and French Constitutions.[42] Generally speaking, Preuss did not have much admiration for the American system. He stuck to what had been regarded as common knowledge since Tocqueville, namely that the presidential system in America had been corrupted by the spoil system and that in the long run it would lead to the intellectual bankruptcy of political life.[43] In the Weimar National Assembly this was not only a prejudice held by Liberals and Conservatives; the Social Democrats were particularly fond of speaking about 'corrupt America'[44] and their deep dislike of a strong president alone was enough for them to regard the system as far from an example for Germany to follow. Friedrich Naumann made little headway with the SPD on the Constitutional Committee with his assertion that the 'presidential idea' was not 'conservative *per se*'. He stated: 'I am convinced that as soon as democratic socialism fully realizes its own force, it will make its way back to those natural laws which must be decisive for all forms of government and which will even be taken on by the presidential idea.'[45] It took a considerable effort to win round those SPD Members who, along with Fischer, followed a left-wing tradition in believing that the post of president was entirely superfluous and dangerous. In short, there is no alternative but to agree with Fraenkel, who observed that the fathers of the Weimar Constitution had failed to form 'an apposite view of the American system of government'[46] and that the presidential system did not even have a large number of supporters among the extreme federalists. Once the parliamentary system of the Weimar Republic moved into a crisis there were many lengthy articles in the political press demanding a strengthening of the president's function and trying to suggest ways of releasing the government from its reliance on fortuitous majorities in parliament.

Once again, it was a period of time when the model of constitutional monarchy was a stronger example than the American constitution. The revisionists called less for a new constitution than for a clarification of the existing Weimar constitution and the prospects for the presidential system in Germany were generally viewed with scepticism, throughout the years of crisis as well.

In *Finland*, the dualist (semipresidential, semiparliamentarian) system was also set up under the influence of the teachings of Duguit and Redslob. The intellectual father of the constitution and subsequently the first president, Ståhlberg, went even further than Redslob when he stated that the intention was that the president would be able to act independently (without his ministers) over important issues.[47] The USA was a much stronger model for work on the Finnish constitution than it had been for the Weimar National Assembly, and Finnish writers attach importance to the point that most of the work on their constitution was done before Weimar, and that it is thus intellectually independent of the Weimar solution. In an interview some time later, Redslob stated that he felt that the Finnish system did indeed embody the ideas in which he believed. For conservative critics (analogous to the German Nationalists in the Weimar National Assembly), however, the Finnish system was not dualist enough. They disapproved of the parliamentary element found in the constitution. As in Germany, there was still a considerable Monarchist minority in Finland, which even managed to get a decision in favour of a monarchist form of government through in October 1918. The collapse of the monarchy in Germany, however, led the candidate, Friedrich Karl von Hessen, to renounce the Finnish Throne. The next parliament elected in April 1919 had a large republican majority. The semipresidential constitutional solution did, however, represent a certain compromise with the Monarchists. This left the Social Democrats as the most determined opponents of this particular solution. Their constitutional expert, Kuusinen, opposed the draft as 'too American' and made counterproposals for a solution along the lines of the Swiss collegial system.[48] The indirect universal election of the president, taken from American presidential practice, also grew out of functional necessities – it was a compromise between the proposal of the Radical Republicans, who desired direct, popular election and the supporters of the election of the President by Parliament.

3   During the third phase of the adoption of American institutions after the Second World War, it was by no means the presidential system on which interest focused most. The point has already been made in the general overview in Chapter 1 that the supporters of the American system were in the minority everywhere, and the American victors themselves did not push their system at all strongly, even in the case of the defeated powers, Germany, Japan and Italy.

The search for constitutional equilibrium in a republic which had still not been consolidated internally also motivated many *Italians* to plead in favour of the presidential system after the Second World War. It is no coincidence that the call for the presidential system was loudest in that country (certainly much louder than in France or Germany), since the constitutional ideas of parliamentary monarchy under the *Statuto Albertino* of 1848 were still very much alive and it was essential to consider the feelings of the substantial monarchist minority outvoted in the referendum. It is true that there were analysts who felt that the difference between the presidential and parliamentary systems of government in a modern 'party state' were not sufficiently important to allow a constitutionalist civil war to develop out of the issue.[49] For many, however, propaganda in favour of the presidential system was a passionate cause. In 1945, Roberto Lucifredi maintained that there was much sympathy for the presidential system in Italy, but he was only very hesitant in recommending it, since he did not wish to forestall the *Constituente*.[50] Because of the risk of dictatorship, Barile, a constitutional lawyer, tended more to favour the Swiss collegial system rather than the presidential one.[51] His teacher, Calamandrei, who wrote the preface to his book, had, however, repeatedly advocated the presidential system. Calamandrei (an *Autonomista*) turned out to be the most competent opponent of parliamentary government during the work on the constitution and he had many an argument with Ruini, the chairman of the Constitutional Commission. Even during the plenary debate in the constituent assembly itself, Calamandrei still tried to cite the deliberations of the second subcommittee, where the presidential form of government had been proposed.[52] Two of that subcommittee's rapporteurs, Mortati and Conti, had dealt with the pros and cons of the presidential system for Italy. Mortati believed that the concentration of power in the hands of the president, as created by the American system, could only be rendered harmless by large-scale decentralization (such as was impossible in Italy).[53] Another member, Einaudi, pointed out that in Latin America not even federalism had proven itself to be a barrier against the collapse of the presidential system into dictatorship.[54] Einaudi also drew attention to the growing criticism among Americans of their own system, and made the assertion that the Americans themselves realized that their system would have to move nearer to the parliamentary one.

Only Calamandrei fought on indefatigably in favour of the presidential system and tried to take the heat out of the fear of dictatorship by pointing out that the Fascist dictatorship in Italy had arisen out of a parliamentary system and not a presidential one.[55] The Left (and La Rocca more than anyone) once again displayed its traditional opposition to a presidential system. When, at the end of the debate, a vote was taken on a motion moved by the Republican, Perassi, calling for a rejection of the presidential system, since 'neither the presidential nor the directory system fitted the conditions of Italian society', the proponents of the presidential system did not even dare to vote openly. The motion was adopted by 22:0 with 6 abstentions.[56] With the acceptance of this decision, the advocates of presidential government had lost the decisive battle – a defeat it was not possible to reverse even in the plenary of the constituent assembly.

After this decision, all that was still possible was a compromise with the proponents of a stronger constitutional influence along Weimar lines. The grand old man of Italian constitutional law, Orlando, was one of the loudest critics of what he saw as the *fannullone* (lit. 'idler') in the president's chair, which is what he believed the Constitutional Committee's proposals involved. Influential individuals in political and academic circles, such as Ruini, Orlando, de Gasperi or Saragat, were in favour of a directly elected president. They were, however, defeated by a majority who wanted to have the president elected by parliament.

The advocates of a popular election of the president were at their strongest in the *gruppo misto*, to which Ruini and Orlando belonged – a fact which did not stop them from arguing fiercely with one another. In Italy, the majority was not even ready to approve of an attempt to combine the advantages of the American and French systems. The failures of the Weimar system repeatedly furnished arguments for the opponents of a presidential constitution.

In *Germany*, the presidential system was also favoured by a number of 'Liberal Conservatives', who hoped it would ensure government stability and equilibrium within the system. As late as the 49th meeting of the main committee of the Parliamentary Council on 9th February 1949, Thomas Dehler demanded that all the preliminary decisions should be reviewed once again and that there should be a new discussion of the presidential system of government, a suggestion, indignantly rejected by Katz, an SPD Member, because all the work already achieved by then would be called in question, since presidential government could not be created by the mere amendment of a few paragraphs in the draft of the Basic Law they had before them.[57] Katz accused Thomas Dehler of 'crying after the *Führer*' and expressed the belief that a presidential system would represent a more serious threat for the young German democracy than an unstable parliamentary government. In the Organizational Committee, Dehler's and Becker's proposals were also supported by a number of CSU members.[58]

On the other hand, it was especially from the conservative side that harsh criticism was levelled against the American system; one example was Schwalber, a CSU member:

> Let me now just comment briefly on the presidential system. The way in which this system operates in the USA is by no means ideal. Should it happen that the presidential system is combined with the highly suggestive personality of a Roosevelt and with the sort of difficulties which would make it seem wise to elect the same president several times over, then it will lead to such a concentration of power in the hands of the president and his administration as to represent a noticeable undermining of democracy and the serious risk of a policy being pursued which is against the country's vital interests. Of one thing I am completely convinced: the dictatorial style of government of President Roosevelt in the last years of his life, at a time when he was ill and no longer in full command of his faculties of judgement has brought upon the world the tragic state of affairs where, in military terms, America most definitely won the war, beyond the slightest trace of a doubt, but where, politically, the struggle against the enemy of freedom, who still exists today, is already basically as good as lost. Politically speaking, the most optimistic view at present would be that of a stalemate. This disastrous development is due primarily to the fact that a President, who had governed for many years with

virtually no check at all, and who was certainly no longer fully in command of all his faculties, so grossly misjudged the situation in Teheran and Yalta, as would not have been possible, had he been subject to effective parliamentary scrutiny. Let me add another thought, by way of an aside: the radical treatment prescribed for Germany in the form of the Morgenthau Plan and its fateful effects on our country can only be explained at all in terms of this exaggeration of the presidential principle.[59]

Given the general lack of precise information in Germany at that time regarding the true political objectives of the allied victors, rumours as to what they intended were repeatedly brought into the debate, on occasions in the form of heated arguments against the American model. Once the proponents of the presidential system had been defeated, they directed their efforts to stabilizing the government, mainly by means of the constructive vote of no-confidence. On many occasions, this solution was branded as a 'substitute for the presidential system'.

It is obvious that the Americans tried not to intervene in the conflict between those proposing a parliamentary system and advocates of presidential government. The Allies' requirements and objections concentrated primarily on federalism. It would also have been extremely difficult to get a majority in the three Allies in favour of a presidential system. A number of individuals among Clay's advisers (such as Carl Joachim Friedrich) repeatedly propounded the advantages of introducing the presidential system to German politicians but no actual pressure was brought to bear over this issue.[60]

4   *France* is a special case of the introduction of a semipresidential system. What was primarily at stake here was *reestablishing the balance between president and parliament.*

When the constitution of the Fourth Republic was drawn up, propaganda in favour of a presidential system had had very little effect, although there were also a number of political writers in France who recommended a presidential system for the new constitution. In the *Résistance* only one conservative group, around Blocq-Mascart in 1943, had propagated a variation on the presidential constitution.[61] It was not coincidental that when the Fourth Republic collapsed Blocq-Mascart again started writing in favour of a semipresidential system and was an ardent defender of de Gaulle's plans against the suspicious parliamentarians on the consultative constitutional committee of 1958. During the war a number of different writers, such as Jacques Maritain and Léon Blum, showed leanings towards a derived form of the presidential idea. In a frequently quoted passage from 1941, Blum expressed himself in rather vague terms: '*J'encline, pour par ma part, vers les sys-*

tèmes du type américain ou helvétique, qui se fondent sur la séparation et l'équilibre des pouvoirs' ('As far as I am concerned, I tend towards systems of the American or Swiss type, based on the separation and equilibrium of powers').[62] After the war, Blum made a speedy return to the idea of parliamentary government, which predominated in his party, and to the subject of reform, on which he had already made a name for himself in articles written during the interwar years. This return to a belief in the parliamentary system was influenced in Blum's case not least by distrust of de Gaulle, of whom it was said (not entirely fairly) that he had a predilection for the presidential system. Writing in *Populaire* on 9th October 1946, Blum stated that de Gaulle himself was the weightiest single argument against the constitutional regime he was proposing.[63] De Gaulle's major opponent in the second presidential election of 1965, François Mitterand, was to repeat the same argument. In giving an assessment of the presidential system, he came to the conclusion that Gaullism had compromised it, since its implicit dangers would be measured in terms of de Gaulle's government practice.

The constitutional plans of the parties and individual members submitted to the two national constituent assemblies of 1946 represented variations of the parliamentary constitution. Only the draft drawn up by the outsider, Jean-Pierre Giraudoux, had taken up the idea of borrowing from both the Swiss and American systems in a combination which demonstrated a degree of authority rarely encountered. When Giraudoux' proposals were rejected by all the parties on 11 April 1946, he reacted by saying: '*Je sais que ma Constitution ne sera celle de la IVe République. Je me console en me disant qu'elle sera peut-être celle de la Ve.*' ('I know that my constitution is not going to be that of the Fourth Republic but I seek consolation in the thought that it may perhaps be that of the Fifth.')[64] With hindsight, as of 1958, the obstinacy of this defeated outsider was to take on an unexpected element of prophesy.

The agitation of Gaullists, such as René Capitant or Michel Debré, against the Constitution of the Fourth Republic did not include direct campaigning for a presidential system. De Gaulle's famous speech in Bayeux, which became the rallying call for 'revisionists' and those unhappy in the Fourth Republic, also contained some basic elements of the 1958 system but not the advocacy of the American system, of which de Gaulle was frequently accused. The confusion over similar words which already existed in German in distinguishing between '*präsidentielles System*' (presidential system) and '*Präsidialregierung*' (presidential government), became even worse in French, with a single term, '*régime présidentiel*' often used to cover both. The contradictory concepts of a 'presidential' or 'parliamentary' constitution went so far as to influence votes even on technical points of detail. Just before a vote that was to decide the fate of his government in spring 1947, Prime Minister

Ramadier stated: 'The parliamentary regime has been contrasted with the presidential one. I urge everyone in favour of the presidential regime to vote against me'.[65]

After the collapse of the Fourth Republic there were not a few Frenchmen who feared that de Gaulle would establish a presidential system. When de Gaulle submitted his plans at a gathering of chairmen of the parliamentary groups of the political parties during preliminary discussions on 31 May 1958, many were relieved that de Gaulle did not want to abolish the parliamentary element altogether and that his call was for a consistently dualist system. The pro-parliamentarians, who were granted only very little latitude to express their opinions on the consultative constitutional committee and no chance at all of impeding the government's plans, still fought bitterly against individual aspects borrowed from the American system. The strengthening of the president was accepted without much of a struggle, especially since de Gaulle initially renounced direct election. Paul Reynaud, Coste-Floret and Teitgen focused their struggle against the incompatibility between the mandate of a deputy and ministerial office.

It has often been asked why de Gaulle did not make more of a break with the traditional pattern of separation of powers on that occasion. The intellectual father of the 1958 Constitution, Michel Debré, explained in a speech delivered to *the Conseil d'Etat* (Council of State) as Minister of Justice on 27 August 1958 why there had been no plans for the introduction of a full presidential constitution: 'The qualities of the presidential system are self-evident . . . but neither the Parliament in its willingness to carry through a reform, as expressed in the law of 3 June, nor the government in submitting and later in applying this law, fell victim to such a temptation and I believe it was an act of wisdom'.[66] Foreign observers interpreted de Gaulle's and Debré's considerations as meaning that de Gaulle could not yet dare to make a complete break with France's parliamentary tradition.[67] The arbitrary amendment to the constitution in 1962, which introduced direct popular election of the president, helped to fuel the assumptions that de Gaulle had had further-reaching plans from the very beginning but had postponed them owing to public opinion. It cannot be ruled out that Debré exercised the biggest single influence over this decision. The books he wrote during the Fourth Republic convey the impression that he himself tended more towards 'Orleanist parliamentarism' than to a full presidential system. Debré himself justified his resignation in 1962 in terms of opposition to the planned amendment to the constitution, whilst trying to prevent harming de Gaulle personally. Despite such moderation, there was always a suspicion in 1958 that de Gaulle wanted to make the ministers dependent on the president and not on parliament. There was a major controversy over the alternatives '*président qui préside ou président qui gouverne'* (A president who chairs or a president who governs). De Gaulle answered such questions from members of the constitutional committee entirely in the sense of parliamentary government. He did admittedly defend the right of dissolution without the countersignature of the government but denied that there would be a twofold, simultaneous responsibility of ministers to the President and to Parliament, which could lead *de facto* to the presidential system.[68] The right of the President to dissolve Parliament without the government's countersignature, which is something the German Nationalists had been demanding back in the days of the Weimar National Assembly, remained strangely intact in the commission's recommendations (despite the resistance of individual pro-parliamentary members). In that way, the advocates of parliamentary government had, themselves, given up one important point in the rules of the system. This type of constitution was, however, not presidential, since dissolution cannot be combined with the presidential system. The pro-parliamentary members would, however, presumably not have made such concessions had they suspected that the Constitution would be amended in favour of a directly elected President only a few years later.

De Gaulle himself was no friend of a fully presidential system along American lines. At a press conference held on 31 January 1964 he spoke against the merging of the offices of head of state and head of government, which would be an automatic part of the presidential system. In doing so, he evidenced the dangers of a complete deadlock between the powers in the event of an obstruction by Parliament, which would inevitably lead to the general paralysis of the system, where only two courses of action would remain open to the president: *pronunciamento* or resignation. It was this last option which caused him the greater horror.[69] De Gaulle was realistic enough to see that in the current system he would have a considerably stronger position than he could have had in the presidential system.

Since the 1962 constitutional amendment, many of the critics of the 1958 constitution have also gone over to the pro-presidential camp. Once upon a time, 'revision' was the motto of right-wing groups in the Third and Fourth Republic; the Left, on the other hand had always maintained a deep distrust of any revisionist plans, despite the large number of objections they had to a constitution with strong inbuilt conservative features. Later on the revision of the constitution to bring in a fully presidential system was even advocated by people politically to the left of the Gaullists. Duverger, who had been a vehement critic of the Constitution in 1958, was one of them.[70] Despite that, many people overestimated the 'presidential movement'. It is not only the Communists who appear to be pretty immune to the thought of a presidential constitution.[71] Most Socialists were also opponents of the presidential system. In answering an opinion survey, André Philip maintained that the presidential system was neither stable nor effective and he called it the weakest government of all, whereas Jules Moch stuck more to the traditional prejudice that the belief in a presidential system was more in the tradition of a Bonaparte, a Boulanger, or a Poujade. The Left's candidate for the presidency in 1965, François Mitterand, denied that his candidature represented an implicit recognition of the semi-presidential system and he tried to keep himself out of the argument between advocates of a presidential system and parliamentarists. It was his view that the struggle between the two groups merely lost sight of the main objective of the moment, i.e. forming a common front against the current power in France, which, as he put it, was neither 'parliamentarian' nor 'presidential'.[72] Gaston Deferre was the only Socialist who made concrete proposals for changes to the existing system. His suggested amendments included shortening the President's period in office to five years, to run concurrently with the life of a legislature (-thereby making it clear to the electors that the President needed the cooperation of a majority in Parliament), the abolition of Article 16, limiting the use of the referendum, and, finally, the creation of a genuine *conseil constitutionel*. Basically, however, he appeared to endorse a number of aspects of the existing constitution.

The rejection of the idea of increasing the presidential component in the 1958 constitution was not limited to the Left and paradoxically, the most impassioned plea against the presidential system and for the parliamentary one came from Tixier-Vignancour. Along similar lines to the conservative *Indépendants*, Tixier appealed for the existing constitution to be applied, in accordance with the motto 'bonne ou mauvaise, elle est ma loi' (it's my law, good or bad').[73] Only the MRP member, Coste-Floret, who had been one of the most influential politicians in the constituent bodies of 1946 and 1958, declared himself in favour of the 'personalization of power' and the 'simplification of politics', by giving the electors the opportunity of making a clear decision in favour of one person in the presidential system. Writers of such different persuasions as the philosopher Gabriel Marcel, or the editor-in-chief of *Le Monde*, Jacques Fauvet, were sceptical about the presidential system. Georges Vedel had warned earlier on against the '*mythologie du régime présidentiel*' (mythology of the presidential system).

It transpired that, for many, campaigning in favour of the presidential system represented 'taking the bull by the horns'. The semi-presidential system of the Fifth Republic had taken power away from parliament. Several saw a chance that a rigorous separation of powers, which is an inherent part of the presidential system, might lead to an improvement in the status of Parliament.[73] It was remembered that the presidential system had often been called 'the presidential-congressional' system. There was, however, a fear that the introduction of the American system would simply mean the continuation of Gaullist illusions without de Gaulle, once de Gaulle himself had gone. Even in the current system where (according to de Gaulle's own conviction) the position of the president is stronger than in the American system, the absolutely dominant position of the president has not had the salutary consequences its advocates had hoped as regards the party system, voting patterns and parliamentary *mores*. At all events, it can safely be stated that de Gaulle could hardly have been less appropriate to serve as a model for President in the American system. The American-style president must strengthen his own position as party leader in order to bridge the gulf between Congress and the government. De Gaulle's antiquated contempt for the party state even allowed his own membership of the party to become the party's symbol of integration against his will. Instead of putting his charisma as a national hero to the test as the leader of a modern party, bringing together the Right, which had been traditionally split in France, de Gaulle used his organizational talent to serve an ideology of specialization, combined with an approach of 'divide and rule' in party politics. It may be that for the duration of his period in office, the French President was repeatedly able to succeed in appearing as *deus ex machina* and throwing the weight of his personal prestige into the balance in order to push his policy through Parliament and the government. With such government tactics, however, it was not possible to build up a system capable of outliving the person concerned.

De Gaulle's return to the semidualist system was less inspired by the presidential system than by the Orleanist-type pre-parliamentary constitutional dualism. Under de Gaulle, the claim to have a monopoly of representing the nation occasionally led to the sort of phenomena which had once made politics difficult in constitutional monarchies: for instance, when the majority in parliament felt itself to be in opposition. In a pure parliamentary system, the sort of opposition which the president of the Senate, Monnerville, tried to organize in 1962 would be scarcely conceivable.

It was not until the parliamentary election of March 1986 that there was once again talk of a new crisis in the semipresidential system. The UDF and RPR together wanted to do a 'Macmahon' on Mitterand. Using the historical precedent, they threatened that in the event of their victory, he would have to '*se soumettre ou se démettre*' (yield or resign). The 'cohabitation' of different majorities would be made impossible right at the outset by individual components refusing to cooperate in a coalition. That, in turn, represents the beginning of a renewed discussion on the possibility of transforming the Fifth Republic into a full presidential system. This is precisely what earlier experts regarded as impossible. To begin with, no less an authority on France than Stanley

Hoffmann regarded the regime moving back towards a parliamentary system as more likely.[74] However, the 'internal logic of the system' was often put forward as an argument in favour of 'presidentializing' it. The 1981 change in power appeared to have halted this development. In 1964, Mitterand had branded the gradual expansion of the powers of the President as a 'permanent *coup d'état*'.[75] As of 1974, the candidate of the Left has adjusted one step at a time to the presidential idea and the supremacy of the President.[76] Since 1981, he has even reacted in a more Gaullist fashion than de Gaulle himself over certain issues. For the eventuality of two hostile majorities, even the Socialists are, once again, beginning to reopen the discussion on complete 'presidentialization' of the system. Without showing any enthusiasm for the American system, Guy Mollet had, in resignation, once suggested removing the hybrid element by letting the people choose between two models, a parliamentary one and a presidential one[77] – a well-meaning proposal but one which would certainly have demanded too much of the people and could, under certain circumstances have left the decision regarding the system to short-lived majorities. The left wing, as represented by Pierre Mauroy, is still strictly against a full presidential system.[78] The electoral reform of 1985, a return to proportional representation in Parliament, must, on the other hand, be seen as a step towards parliamentary government.

European political scientists have become cautious about hazarding a forecast as to the effects of institutional reforms. In the semi-presidential systems, which have not taken over all the aspects of American institutions, clear disproportions can be seen between the powers of the directly elected president derived from the constitution and what happens in reality, given the constraints of the party system and the strength of parliament:

Presidential Power			
Order of countries according to the constitution		*Order of countries in political reality*	
1	Finland	1	France
2	Iceland	2	Finland
3	Weimar	3	Weimar
4	Portugal	4	Portugal
5	Austria	5	Austria
6	France	6	Ireland
7	Ireland	7	Iceland

Source: Maurice Duverger: *Le système politique français*, Paris, PUF 1985, 18th edition, p. 522.

The only way of closing this gap would be to give in to the *'tentation américaine'* ('American temptation'), something often mentioned in French literature, without there being any real give in practice.

The Failure of the Presidential System in the Third World

The American model has repeatedly suffered setbacks in its international image as a result of the failure of the presidential system in Latin America. Because of experience in South America, the rumour spread that it was likely to collapse into dictatorship. Most South American states have answered the threats not by turning away from the model but trying mechanical means of coping with potential dictatorship. The simplest method seemed to be to place a rigid restriction on the president's right to re-election but occasionally the best of intentions produced too much of a good thing. In Chile, the impossibility of re-electing President Frei in 1970 contributed in no small way to the collapse of the system, since presumably Allende would not have been able to hold his own against a candidate like Frei.

The cases where experiments were carried out on different systems are few and far between; one is *Brazil* in the 1960s. The retreat from the experiment with the alternative, parliamentary system was so rapid that it is not possible to draw a genuine comparison regarding the performance of the two competing models of democracy in that country. On 29 August 1961, a committee of the Brazilian Congress approved a proposal to bring in a parliamentary form of government to replace the presidential one and on 31 August Congress as a whole adopted the proposal. Ex-President Kubitschek voted no, since the change in the constitution had been blackmailed out of the executive. President Goulart, who had been abroad at the time of the 'coup' and was faced with a *fait accompli*, gave his blessing to the amendment to the constitution in a radio broadcast on 3 September. The ministers responsible for the army, navy and air force were obliged to recommend their troops to bow to the 'sovereign decision' of congress. On 7 September, Goulart was sworn in as president and, on the next day, the Social Democrat, Tancredo Neves, became the first parliamentary Prime Minister. The system suffered a serious setback when the second Prime Minister designate, Dantas, failed in the vote of investiture on 28 June 1962, and the third Prime Minister, Brochado, was forced to resign on 13 September, because the majority of his government was not ready to make a confidence issue out of the planned referendum on the existence of the parliamentary system. The criticism of the parliamentary system grew stronger rapidly, and on 7 January 1963 the reintroduction of the presidential system was approved in the referendum with 4.8

million votes in its favour against 912 000 votes cast for the parliamentary system. President Goulart himself had campaigned in favour of the presidential system.[79] The long period of government by the military has, however, rendered this episode of little value for comparing the *modus operandi* of the parliamentary and presidential system within a single country.

So far there has been no successful adoption of the presidential system outside the United States. Nonetheless, it is essential to warn against using that as sufficient evidence of the inadequacy of the presidential system. The reference to South America is particularly shaky, since the South American systems (in common with attempts to introduce the presidential system in South Korea, the Philippines or Liberia) all had to develop under the sort of social conditions that would have jeopardized any form of modern representative democracy.[80] The parliamentary systems did not work satisfactorily in South America either, and it has been repeatedly judged that the presidential system in South America has stood up comparatively well.[81] Experiences with the parliamentary system in Chile or Bolivia, on the other hand, have often been viewed as pretty negative.[82]

The Chilean politician, Arturo Alessandri, who published a hymn of praise to the presidential system, managed to become the initiator of a reform movement in Chile in which the executive's dependence on votes in parliament was abolished. In numerous South American countries the choice was in favour of a hybrid form between the two systems, that of the 'President in the Council of Ministers' and the parliamentary component was strengthened to avoid *caudillismo*.[83] Nowhere, however, did this hybrid form develop as a hindrance to the president. Since the presidential election is normally held at the same time as the parliamentary one, the latter is completely overshadowed by the former. Patronage and threats are means available to the president to secure a majority in the legislature for the future as well but the use of parliamentary measures, such as censure motions against ministers appointed by the president, often turned out to be mere preliminaries to a *pronunciamento* against the president himself.[84]

This episode sparked off the publication of a large number of pamphlets for and against the presidential system. Raul Pilla, who was one of the leading pro-parliamentarians to urge an amendment to the constitution during the crisis of the summer of 1961, had made his views known in a book published back in 1958, where he attempted to prove the superiority of the parliamentary system over the presidential.[79] Brazil's first Prime Minister, Tancredo Neves, also thought the parliamentary system was the more appropriate and democratic for his country.[85] The defenders of a presidential system made the point that Brazil's federal structure could be better combined with this[86] – an argument sufficiently familiar from anti-parliamentarian literature in Europe. In addition, it was claimed that the parliamentary system was only suitable for small countries and that larger territories were better off with the presidential system. A further point, it was maintained, was that the presidential system would bring benefits in terms of planning to a developing country like Brazil. Stability of government irrespective of fluctuations in public opinion was put forward as a further advantage. In the same way, the presidential system was held to represent an ideal half-way solution between a developing-country dictatorship and constitutional separation of powers. The assumption was frequently made that parliamentary government required as a *sine qua non* a higher degree of development than Brazil had attained in the sixties.[87]

In the process, rational lines of argument in favour or against the presidential system played the least significant part. The two forms of government were used as arguments in the power struggle between groups and there was no shortage of attempts to discriminate against the parliamentary form of government as a 'communist plot' against the 'good old order of things' which was introduced by Varga back in 1946. Throughout this constitutional struggle, the military adopted a basic attitude of 'wait and see'.[88]

It is only to a limited extent that the failure of attempts to transplant the presidential system to developing countries can be ascribed to the system itself. What appears to be much more dangerous than the institutions of the presidential system is the predominant way in which leading politicians are recruited in developing countries which have just achieved independence. Only a small group has any real chance of success. Only politicians who have been leaders of the liberation movement manage to establish themselves and there is a general tendency for competition for power to be organized only on a very incomplete basis over a period of decades. Brogan has pointed out that this does not represent a new drawback to the presidential system. It was not until 1837 that van Buren became the first President of the United States to have had no direct links with the American Revolution. In the United States political competition was also only partial for several decades as a result of the hasty departure of Tories for Canada or England.[89] The resultant dangers are by no means less under a non-presidential system. It is possible to see stronger barriers to the usurpation of power to the presidential system than to the parliamentary one. Transplantation attempts in Africa and South America have, however, left out a whole series of the safeguards against the abuse of power, which were either built in by the founding fathers or emerged later as a result of the dynamic political process (for example the strengthening of the Supreme Court).

The overall assessment of dualist constitutions is made more difficult by the fact that only one case which has grown up historically has survived. This is why organicistic prejudices against the constitutional transplantations are particularly widespread in judgements on dualist constitutions. Once the ideology of 'genuine British parliamentarism' had faded, political writers became accustomed to recognizing that the basic features of the parliamentary system could indeed be transplanted but that they were subject to considerable functional modifications in the various countries. Today nobody would still challenge that a parliamentary system with a President chosen by indirect popular election, such as the Finnish one, has demonstrated its vitality, despite numerous difficulties. Israel has implemented parliamentary government without the right to dissolve parliament which is normally regarded as a *conditio sine qua non* of the system; on the other hand, the Netherlands have moved towards parliamentary government – whilst maintaining the incompatibility between representative mandate and ministerial office. We simply do not have such experience of the possible variations on the theme of the presidential system. Political publications in America are still steeped in antiquated claims, such as that the parliamentary system is an exotic plant in America and, as such, cannot thrive under the social conditions prevalent on that continent.[90] This claim can readily be discounted by citing the case of Canada. Nobody will deny that Canada (with the possible exception of Quebec) shows similar social conditions to the United States and is even comparable to the USA as regards its federal structure. Australia could also be brought in for the purposes of comparison – which has been done far too little to date in comparative literature. Whereas empirical evidence is available today to disprove the claim that a parliamentary government is not capable of surviving in North America, the counter claim, that the presidential system cannot survive in Europe, has so far only had doubt shed on it in the form of partial analyses and assumptions.

Concluding Remarks

The failure or the functional changes in the transfer of individual institutions of the presidential system have often been misused to reach a value judgement on the American system of democracy as a whole. Presumably, the prejudice that presidential government could not take root in Europe on account of the greater fragmentation of societies is less untenable than the claim that the parliamentary system of government could not survive in America. In the event of a trial run, what would matter most would be *which* parliamentary system could be most meaningful for America.

The mere fact that the presidential system might be able to survive in

Europe is, of itself, however, not an adequate reason for recommending it to European countries. The main argument against it is that some of the salutary effects that critics of the parliamentary system promise themselves from the presidential system either do not appear to be desirable to many people or would not necessarily occur in Europe anyway. At this juncture, it is necessary to discuss a series of points on which the presidential system is often portrayed in literature as being superior to the parliamentary one.

1   In periods where foreign-policy considerations predominate, it is claimed that the presidential system is more likely to achieve foreign-policy goals and possesses greater flexibility in warding off threats.[91] It is an argument used in comparisons with the parliamentary system. Tocqueville, in his comparison of the presidential system and constitutional monarchy, regarded the fact that the American President was elected by the people, as actually being a source of instability and agitation, which could only be afforded by a country far away from the world's foreign-policy conflicts.[92]

In France, the argument of the foreign-policy authority of the directly elected President has become popular once again through that country's big-power nuclear policy. Back in 1964, Goguel stated that the nuclear threat of the major powers called for immediate decisions and could not wait for cabinet deliberations. In his view, the presidential system is able to cope with this problem of the modern state better than the parliamentary cabinet system.[93] During the wartime conferences frequent observations were made regarding the link between the system of government and foreign-policy decisions. At the Atlantic conference, Hopkins could only see the positive side to the presidential system: Roosevelt was able to take a decision on his own. Churchill, on the other hand, had to remain constantly in touch with the War Cabinet and especially with Lord Privy Seal Attlee in London. In that connection, it has been correctly pointed out that the American President's greater room for manoeuvre went hand-in-hand with a greater degree of isolation, which was all too easily compensated with the assistance of unaccountable advisers in the 'kitchen cabinet'. No one will say that the presidential system stood up better in the war. In its own way, Churchill's leadership was just as effective as Roosevelt's, even if, for tactical reasons (such as in Yalta), Churchill played up the idea that he was the only accountable head of government at the conference, using his dependence on parliament to delay overhasty decisions. Wilson's naively doctrinaire stance at Versailles or that of Roosevelt in Yalta cannot, however, be explained in terms of America's system of government alone. But it is likely that a parliamentary head of government would have had to pay more attention to the mood back home, and this would not only have had a beneficial effect on the possibility of implementing foreign policy but also on the quality of the decisions taken.

During the First World War, the parliamentary system in France and Belgium stood up to serious crises surprisingly well. The presidential system has not so far been subject to such make-or-break foreign-policy trials on this scale. No one would wish for such a test today, which would be tantamount to nuclear war, but it may reasonably be assumed that the presidential system would also react satisfactorily to increased demands. That, alone, does not, however, permit any conclusion regarding the superiority of this system of government in terms of foreign-policy decisions.

2   The most popular advantage of the presidential system is that it creates stable governments for long periods of time. This has become the most important motive for advocates of the presidential system in Europe. It is, however, not an argument which would permit a clear-cut conclusion as regards the superiority of the presidential system either.

It is possible to make several objections to the argument of government stability. One view of the presidential system often focuses in a biased manner on the continuity of the office of president. Inadequate attention is paid to the discontinuity of secretaries of state or the leading government offices under the president. Under some presidents, rotation of office has taken on dimensions virtually unknown since ancient times. Parliamentary systems with a loosely-knit party structure also show large-scale rotation of office but the stability of cabinet membership as a whole is comparatively high, despite changes in the head of government and continuous ministerial reshuffles. The semipresidential system of the Fifth French Republic has already had the same effect on continuity in office as the American system. Of the membership of the first cabinet of 1 January 1959, only two ministers, Jacquinot and Couve de Murville, were still in office in 1965. Of the 27 ministers and under-secretaries of state in the Debré government of 9 January 1959, only two still had the same function in 1965 (Malraux and Couve de Murville) and only three remained, albeit in other posts (Jacquinot, Giscard D'Estaing and Maurice-Bekanowski). All the other 22 had already been replaced. Of the 29 members of the Pompidou government of April 1962, ten had already disappeared by 1965 and another five had changed jobs. Jules Moch, who introduced these figures as part of his argument against a presidential system, quite rightly expressed his doubts as to whether the continuity and effectiveness of the semipresidential system was greater than that in the parliamentary regime. It is to be feared that this trend will become worse, if parliamentary accountability is replaced by accountability to the president alone.

3   It is often said of the presidential system coupled to majority voting in elections that it makes 'alternative government' easier. American history teaches us, however, that the cycles of change in government tend to have somewhat longer phases than those in the parliamentary system, although there have been heads of government, particularly in parliamentary countries, who have remained in office for very long periods of time, such as MacKenzie King in Canada, Menzies in Australia, Ben Gurion in Israel, Adenauer in Germany, de Gasperi in Italy, Erlander in Sweden and Gerhardsen in Norway. But, the benefits of government stability and continuity also have drawbacks. It is far from true that the most stable governments have always been the best, and it would be a dire mistake to make a fetish of stability as the most desirable constitutional asset in representative democracies. In America's presidential system, the stable executive plus changing majorities in the 'midterm elections' has threatened to have particularly negative consequences, but that is not a general objection to the presidential system. A successful attempt to transfer the system would presumably be one without these midterm elections.

In this context, the classical argument that the civil service in Europe is more highly developed takes on particular significance once again. The long-established tradition and the strict rules governing civil service recruitment have the effect, in most parliamentary states in Europe, of making discontinuity at the head of the executive less serious than it would be otherwise.

4   It is said that the presidential system encourages a trend towards the two-party system. Given the plethora of rules set up by the electoral laws of the individual states, it is very difficult to draw a generally valid dividing line between the significance of the American electoral system and that of the presidential system. A presidential system in Europe without general elections based on a relative majority would presumably not give rise to any tendency towards the two-party system. Even the French system, with two rounds of polling, does not permit the advantages of majority electoral law to take full effect. A number of observers, however, have ascribed to the primaries in some American states an effect which is at least similar to that of majority voting with two rounds. The studies on the primaries so far available are inadequate to permit such generalizations. In a comparison of individual states before and after the introduction of primaries, V.O. Key has established radical changes in the leadership and behaviour of the parties as a result of their introduction. The effect of the two-ballot electoral system in a multi-party setup, however, has features which can hardly be compared to the institution of primaries in the American states with a two-party system. The polarization in the two-party system is by no

64

means solely dependent on either the electoral–law institutions or the system of government. In the past, it used to be popular to stress the higher level of Anglo-Saxon political culture as the most important reason.

No assessment of the effects of the presidential system on party structure can afford to ignore the electoral college. It is not, however, necessarily essential to view this as being directly linked to the presidential system. It is precisely the institution of the electoral college that could have led to the formation of splinter groups in America and, were there a deeply-rooted multi-party system, the electors would not enter into alliances to facilitate the formation of majorities but would presumably (as provided for in the American Constitution) refer every presidential vote to the House of Representatives. In his day, Tocqueville was still maintaining that the American system for electing the president did not foster integration but rather '*ambitions particulières*' (individual ambitions).[94]

5   It is alleged that the presidential system permits more effective control over government. The parliamentary form of government with its tight grip on powers makes parliament more and more subordinate to the government. This belief is linked in part to an erroneous view of the parliamentary system, 'Cabinet is the committee to end all committees, it can tolerate no rivals',[95] and the power of the Prime Minister is exaggerated in exactly the same way as we tend to exaggerate the supposed risk of dictatorship in the presidential system. The price paid for the stronger parliamentary control in the presidential system is that of antagonism between the powers. It is only if measured in terms of the constitutionally liberal ideal of the nineteenth century, which aimed at as weak a state as possible, that the dualist presidential system would merit priority.

6   It is a widely held opinion that the presidential system offers better protection against arbitrary acts by the majority and is particularly appropriate for countries with large regional and functional differences in the population. Here again, the line of argument has come full circle in the course of history. In the days when parliamentary government, then still in the form of constitutional monarchy, was compared with the presidential system, it was regarded as superior to the republican-dualist system, since the Prince, who in constitutional doctrine represented a '*pouvoir neutre*', afforded better protection against arbitrary acts by the majority than did the popularly elected president, who for Tocqueville (in his analysis of President Jackson's government practice) counted as the very incarnation of majority despotism. Today, many Americans point out that the accusation of majority tyr-

anny is much more applicable to the parliamentary system. In England, the two-party structure coupled with the 'first-past-the-post' electoral system led to major fluctuations in policy in the postwar years, with changing majorities nationalizing or reprivatizing branches of basic industry and hence causing damage to the economy as a result of constant restructuring. It is rightly pointed out that such extreme effects of majority decisions need not be feared in the presidential system. In this objection, the British model is simply equated with the parliamentary system *per se*. Nearly all continental countries have introduced a system where arbitration of conflict among parties whose strength is proportional to the votes cast for them plays a bigger role than does majoritization. Nonetheless, there is a decisive distinction between the parliamentary and the presidential system. Fritz Münch once exaggerated the case by saying: 'Parliamentary government has no purpose, unless it is to be made available to a political movement. Where all that is called for is administration and conservation, where slow reforms are sufficient, then the democratic demand will be satisfied by the American or the Swiss system.'[96] This statement also follows British parliamentary practice too slavishly and ignores the multiplicity of cases of arbitration in other parliamentary systems. At the same time, it cannot be denied that the parliamentary system of government represents a more pliable instrument for the expansion of the modern state supplying extensive services to its citizens. The presidential system, on the other hand, with its complicated system of checks and balances offers much more resistance to any dynamic movement of the parties in government. This explains, in part, why many Liberal-Conservatives have a preference for the presidential system but, at the same time, it also justifies the preference given to the parliamentary system by those groups for whom dynamic socio-political development is more important than the constitutional maintenance of the established order.

Today, the old, highly essentialist debates about the superiority of the presidential system have been overtaken by events. For a long time, it has been becoming increasingly clear that the differences between the presidential and the parliamentary system are of secondary importance.

Bertrand de Jouvenel has already recast the trend towards the 'neo-presidential system' in all representative democracies in terms of a theory about the executive (and by analogy to the constitutional developments in Ancient Rome) he sees an evolution towards princedom in all systems.[97] Despite this functional rapprochement of the representative systems, major differences do still remain between them.

As old as the hybrid forms themselves, is the debate regarding their 'true nature'. The current discussion surrounding the semipresidential systems with a directly elected president is, however, taking place with no regard whatsoever for the presidential system in the USA.[98] In Italy it was the Socialists who launched the debate about a change in the system. Reform of electoral law and a unicameral system show no signs of being inspired by the American model. The 'presidentialization' of the system, which is occasionally discussed, however, takes the Fifth French Republic as its model, and not the USA.[99]

Notes

Parts of this chapter are taken from: *Das präsidentielle Regierungssystem der Vereinigten Staaten in der Lehre der Herrschaftsformen*, Karlsruhe, C.F. Müller, 1967.

1   Carl J. Friedrich: *Man and his Government*, New York, McGraw Hill, 1963, p. 188f.
2   Alexis de Tocqueville: *De la Démocratie en Amérique*, ed J.P. Mayer, Paris, Gallimard, 1961, Vol. 1, p. 132.
3   Robert von Mohl: *Enzyklopädie der Staatswissenschaften*, Tübingen 1872, p. 108. The term is not yet given in the first edition of 1859.
4   Robert von Mohl: *Die Bestellung der ausübenden Gewalt in der repräsentativen Demokratie*, in: *Staatsrecht, Völkerrecht und Politik*, (Tübingen 1860), Reprint Graz, Styria, 1962, Vol. 1 (467-497), pp. 484ff.
5   Ibid, pp. 493-535.
6   For instance, recently: Winfried Steffani: Gewaltenteilung im demokratisch-pluralistischen Rechtsstaat. *Politische Vierteljahresschrift*, 1962, (256-282), p. 271.
7   Similarly: Giambattista Rizzo: *La Repubblica presidenziale*, Rome 1944, p. 330.
8   Max Ferrand (ed.): *The Records of the Federal Convention of 1787*, New Haven, Yale UP, Vol. 1, p. 66.
9   Ibid, p. 65.
10   Ibid, p. 68.
11   *The Federalist*, Everyman edition, p. 265.
12   Ibid.
13   Stephen Horn: *The Cabinet and Congress*, New York, Columbia UP, 1960, p. 21; James MacGregor Burns: *Presidential Government*, Boston, Cambridge 1966, p. 18.
14   Alexander H. Stephens: *A Constitutional View of the Late War between the States*, Philadelphia, 1870, Vol. 2, p. 338.
15   Stephen Horn: *The Cabinet and Congress*, New York, Columbia UP, 1960, p. 49.
16   Woodrow Wilson: *Congressional Government. (1885)*. Cleveland, Meridan Book, 1956, p. 187.
17   Henry Hazlitt in: *New York Times* 8.2.1942; Thomas K. Finletter: *Can Representative Government do the job?* New York, 1945; William Yandell Elliott: *The Need for Constitutional Reform*, New York, 1935.
18   Livio Minguzzi: *Governo di gabinetto e governo presidenziale*, Bologna, 1886, p. 359.
19   Don K. Price: The Parliamentary and Presidential Systems. *Public Administration Review*, 1943, pp. 317-334.
20   Hugo Preuss: *Deutschland republikanische Reichsverfassung*, Berlin, 1923, 2nd edn., p. 68.

21 Harold Laski: The Parliamentary and Presidential Systems. *Public Administration Review*, 1944, pp. 347-359. Reprinted in: *Selected Readings for Government 1a*. Harvard University 1960, pp. 194-207.

22 Un deputato (Sidney Sonnino): *Torniamo allo Statuto*. *Nuova Antologia*, 1887, I, Jan. pp. 9ff. Published again in: Nino Valeri (ed.): *La Lotta politica in Italia dall' unità al 1925. Idee e documenti*, Florence 1962, pp. 251-269.

23 cf. Vincenzo Niceli: *Carattere giuridico del governo costituzionale*. Perugia 1894, Chap. V. *Monarchia costituzionale ed il governo presidenziale*, pp. 113ff, esp. 119, 126.

24 Livio Minguzzi: *Governo di Gabinetto e governo presidenziale*, Bologna 1882, pp. 95ff.

25 Don A. Cánovas de Castillo: *Problemas contemporáneas*, Madrid 1890, Vol. III, pp. 109f, 131.

26 Émile de Laveleye: *Le gouvernement dans la démocratie*, Paris 1896, Vol. 2, pp. 120ff, 137.

27 Ernst Fraenkel: *Deutschland und die westlichen Demokratien*, Stuttgart, Kohlhammer, 1964, p. 82.

28 Comité de constitution: *1848, Procès verbaux* (handwritten minutes) Archives nationales, Paris C 918, p. 59.

29 Ibid., p. 69.

30 *Moniteur*, Session 5th October 1848, p. 2725, col. 3.

31 Ibid., p. 2725, col. 2.

32 Alexis de Tocqueville: *Souvenirs*, Oeuvres, Vol. 12, Paris, Gallimard, 1964, p. 209.

33 Frédéric Bastiat: *Parlamentarische Unvereinbarkeiten* (1849). In: *Ausgewählte volkswirtschaftliche und politische Schriften*, Hamburg, 1859, Vol. 2, (94-155) p. 94.

34 Eckhart G. Franz: *Das Amerikabild der deutschen Revolution von 1848/49*, Heidelberg 1958, p. 134; Thomas Ellwein: *Der Einfluss des amerikanischen Bundesverfassungsrechtes auf die Verhandlungen der Frankfurter Nationalversammlung im Jahre 1948/49*, thesis, Erlangen 1950; Anton Schroll: *Der Einfluss der nordamerikanischen Unionsverfassung auf die Verfassung des Deutschen Reiches vom 28. März 1849*, thesis. Tübingen 1913.

35 Christian Carl Josias Bunsen: *Die Deutsche Bundesverfassung und ihr eigenthümliches Verhältnis zu den Verfassungen Englands und der Vereinigten Staaten. Zur Prüfung des Entwurfs der Siebzehn*, Frankfurt/M. 1848, pp. 17, 19.

36 cf. Ellwein: *Der Einfluss*, op. cit. p. 133.

37 Franz Wigard (ed.): *Stenographischer Bericht über die Verhandlungen der deutschen constituirenden Nationalversammlung zu Frankfurt am Main*, 1849, Vol. VIII, 6065, col. 1.

38 Ibid., Vol. I, p. 508, col. 2.

39 Ibid., Vol. I, p. 446, col. 1.

40 *Verhandlungen der verfassunggebenden Deutschen Nationalversammlung*, Vol. 336, *Bericht des Verfassungsausschusses*, Berlin 1920, p. 233, col. 2, p. 231, col. 2.

41 Max Weber: *Deutschlands künftige Staatsform*, in: idem: *Politische Schriften*, Tübingen, Mohr, 1958, 2nd Edn. p. 457.

42 John Viktor Bredt et al.: *Das Werk der Herrn Preuss oder wie soll eine Reichsverfassung nicht aussehen?* Berlin, 1919, p. 9.

43 Preuss, op. cit. p. 68.

44 Heilfron (ed.): *Die Deutsche Nationalversammlung*, Berlin, 1919: Katzenstein, Vol. 4, p. 3587, Wels, Vol. 7, p. 248.

45 *Verhandlungen*, op. cit. (under 40), p. 278, col. 1.
46 Ernst Fraenkel: *Amerika im Spiegel des deutschen politischen Denkens*, Cologne/ Opladen, Westdeutscher Verlag, 1959, p. 43.
47 K. J. Ståhlberg: *Parlamentarismen i Finlands Statsförfattning*, Helsinki, 1927, p. 19.
48 Sven Lindman: *Parlamentarismens införande i Finlands Statsförfattning*, Uppsala, 1935, p. 44.
49 Giambattista Rizzo: *La Repubblica presidenziale*, Rome, 1944, p. 347.
50 Roberto Lucifredi: *L'assemblea costitutente. Che cosa è, che cosa dovra fare*, Milan, 1945, p. 103.
51 Paolo Barile: *Orientamenti per la costituente*, Florence, 1947, p. 74.
52 *Atti dell'Assemblea costituente*, Rome, 1947, Vol. 3, p. 1753, col. 1.
53 *Assemblea costituente. Commissione per la costituzione. Seconda sottocommissione dal 26 luglio 1946 al 30 gennaio 1947*, Rome 1947, p. 82, col. 2.
54 Ibid., p. 103, col. 2.
55 Ibid., p. 119, col. 2.
56 Ibid., p. 102, col. 2, p. 129, col. 2.
57 *Parlamentarischer Rat. Verhandlungen des Hauptausschusses*, Bonn, 1948/49, p. 638.
58 John Ford Golay: *The Founding of the Federal Republic of Germany*, Chicago UP, 1958, pp. 123ff.
59 *Der Parlamentarische Rat 1948/1949. Akten und Protokolle* Vol. 2. *Der Verfassungskonvent auf Herrenchiemsee*. Boppard, Boldt, 1981, pp. 171f.
60 Carl J. Friedrich: Rebuilding the German Constitution. *APSR*, 1949, pp. 461-482, 704-720. In this work Friedrich appears as a critic of excessive interference by the allied powers.
61 Henri Michel/Boris Mirkine-Guetzévitch: *Les idées politiques et sociales de la résistance*, Paris, 1954, p. 275.
62 Léon Blum: *Oeuvres*, Paris, Vol. 2, 1958, p. 469.
63 Léon Blum: *Oeuvres*, Paris, Vol. 3, 1958, p. 315.
64 *Annales de l'assemblée nationale constituente, élue le 21 octobre 1945*, Vol. 4, p. 1965, col. 3.
65 *Keesings Archives*, 1947, p. 1084 A.
66 Michel Debré: La nouvelle constitution. Rfdsp, 1959, No. 1 (7-29), p. 9.
67 Stanley Hoffmann: The French Constitution of 1958. *APSR*, 1959, (332-357), p. 333.
68 *Travaux préparatoires de la Constitution. Avis et débats du comité consultatif constitutionnel*, Paris, 1960, p. 118, col. 1.
69 Pierre Pluchon: Pour ou contre un régime présidentiel. Un enquête. *Révue politique et parlementaire*. (June 1965, pp. 3-14, July/August pp. 11-24, Sept. 1965, pp. 3-12) Part 3, p. 12. cf. also: Pierre Avril: *Un président pour quoi faire?* Paris, 1965, p. 34.
70 Maurice Duverger: *La Ve République et le régime présidentiel*, Paris, 1961, p. 132; Hughes Tay: Le régime présidentiel et la France, Paris, *LGdJ*, 1967, pp. 289ff.
71 Georges Vedel: Vers le régime présidentiel, *Rfdsp*. 1964 (20-32) p. 21.
72 Pluchon, op. cit. Part 3, p. 9.
73 Francois Goguel: Réflexions sur le régime présidentiel. *Rfdsp*, 1962 (289-311) p. 303.
74 Hoffmann, op. cit. p. 333.
75 Francois Mitterand: *Le coup d'état permanent (1964)*, Paris, Juillard, 1984, 2nd edn.

76   Oliver Duhamel: *La gauche et la Ve République*, Paris, PUF, 1980, p. 279.
77   Guy Mollet: *Quinze ans après. La Constitution de 1958*, Paris, A. Michel, 1973, pp. 150ff.
78   Pierre Mauroy: *A gauche*, Paris, A. Michel, 1985, p. 14.
79   Jorge Rainaldo Vanossi: *Presidencialismo y parlamentarismo en el Brasil.* Buenos Aires, 1964, pp. 42ff; Alfonso Arinos de Melo Franco/Raul Pilla: *Presidencialismo ou Parlamentarismo?* Rio de Janeiro, Olympio, 1958, p. 393.
80   Loewenstein called these instances of transfer 'cases of application without conclusive force'. Karl Loewenstein: *Der Staatspräsident*, in: ibid.: *Beiträge zur Staatssoziologie*, Tübingen, Mohr, 1961 (331-396), p. 350.
81   Jacques Lambet: La transposition du régime présidentiel hors des Etats-Unis. Le cas de l'Amérique latine. *Revue française de science politique*, 1963 (577-600), pp. 580, 599.
82   Arturo Alessandri: *Le régime présidentiel*, Paris, Sirey, 1930; Franklin Antezaña Paz: *Le régime parlementaire en Bolivie*, Paris, Domat-Montchrestien, 1933, pp. 142ff.
83   José Miranda: *Reformas y tendencia constitucionales recientes de la America Latina 1945-1956*, Mexico, Instituto de derecho comparado, 1957, p. 278.
84   Martin Needler: Cabinet Responsibility in a presidential system. The Case of Peru. *Parliamentary Affairs*, 1965, No. 2 (156-161), p. 160f.
85   Tancredo Neves: O regime parlamentar e la realidade Brasileira. Belo Horizonte, *Revista Brasileira de Estudios Políticos*, 1962, pp. 37f.
86   Frederico Trotta: *O sistema parlamentar Brasileiro*, Rio de Janeiro, Vecchi, 1961, pp. 50f.
87   Laureiro Junior: *Parlamentarismo e presidencialismo no Brasil*, Rio de Janeiro, 1962; J. C. de Oliveira Torres: *O presidencialismo no Brasil*, Rio de Janeiro, Cruzeiro, 1962, pp. 60ff.
88   Edwin Lieuwen: *Generals vs. Presidents. Neomilitarism in Latin America*, New York, Praeger 1964, p. 98.
89   Denis Brogan: *The Possibilities of the Presidential Systems in Africa*, In: *Parliament as an Export*, London, 1966 (190-207), p. 197.
90   Wilfred E. Binkley: *President and Congress*, New York, Vintage Book, 1962, p. 379.
91   John W. Burgess: *Political Science and Comparative Constitutional Law*, Boston 1896, Vol. 2, p. 13.
92   Alexis de Tocqueville: *De la démocratie en Amérique, Oeuvres complêtes*, Vol. 1, Paris, Gallimard, 1961, p. 133.
93   Francois Goguel: Quelques remarques sur le problême des institutions politiques en France, *Rfdsp*. 1964 (7-19), p. 11.
94   Tocqueville, op. cit. Vol. 1, p. 130.
95   Price, op. cit.
96   Fritz Münch: *Die Bundesregierung*, Frankfurt, 1954, p. 103.
97   Bertrand de Jouvenel: Du principat, *Rfsdp*, 1964 (1053-1086) p. 1054f.
98   Enzo Cheli u.a. Il governo semi-presidenziale in Europa, *Quaderni costituzionali*, 1983, no. 2.
99   Giuliano Amato et al: *Una costituzione per governare. La 'grande riforma' proposta dai socialisti*, Venice, Marsilio, 1981; Critical of the interests behind the Socialist proposals: Gianfranco Pasquino: *Degenerazioni dei partiti e riforme instituzionali*, Bari, Laterza, 1982, pp. 127ff; Giuliano Amato: *Una Repubblica da riformare*, Bologna, Il Mulino, 1980.

3 Federalism

Federalism is occasionally interpreted as a phenomenon born of military necessity. Anyone who now accepts such an interpretation would not view the USA as the cradle of federalism (as older literature frequently does). The old distinction between a confederation and a federal state, however, still lives on under more modern labels: the USA would thus appear, in contrast to Switzerland, to have a modern centralized form of federalism as opposed to the confederate form of the German Empire or the Dutch Estates General, which Riker describes as 'peripheralized federalism'.[1]

Thus it is still correct to say that the modern idea of federalism has been determined by the USA[2] and that, of all the institutions within the American constitutional structure, it is federalism that has had the greatest influence in the world.[3] This influence was all the greater at a time when federalist systems were strongly advised by the constitutional doctrines of the day to adopt additional institutions from the American model in order to ensure that federalism remained workable.

The presidential system has often been seen as a necessary corollary of federalism. In the nineteenth century it appeared that federalism and parliamentarism were incompatible – especially to ideologists of states' rights from Calhoun in America to Max von Seydel in Germany.[4] In the 19th century, all federal states were constructed on a dualist basis and with separation of powers – as a presidential system in America, as a council system in Switzerland and as a constitutional monarchy in Ger-

71

many. In Brazil, those fighting against abolition of the presidential system in 1961 were still using the argument that large territories with a federal structure needed a presidential system.[5] Similar arguments were used by some of Clay's advisers, such as Carl Joachim Friedrich, to propose the presidential system for Germany. In the case of the European Community, Friedrich even reached the conclusion that 'The more detailed review of executive systems appears to confirm the conclusion that some kind of Council System is best adopted to a multinational federated community'.[6] To put it in the terms of the old (and generally fruitless) debate: for federations, a presidential-type system seemed advisable and for confederations, the Swiss council system.

For those countries of Europe that were composed of different states, such as Switzerland, Italy and Germany, America had a great deal of attraction. Federalism was praised as an 'American invention' and the North American Union was occasionally recognized as having a 'mission'. The Italian writer, Gabriele Rosa, went so far as to compare the significance of the American-type federal republic with the constitutional form of Ancient Rome:

> In the same way as Rome imposed the seal of its laws and its cosmopolitan culture on the Old World around the Mediterranean, so the federal democracy of the USA will become the predominant type in a new political era for humanity.[7]

It was, however, precisely *Italy* which turned out to be the country where setting up the state was a veritable *debellatio*, on account of Piedmont's supremacy. Even Prussia, with a position of hegemony in the post-1871 German Empire, had to be more considerate of the other member states than was Piedmont. For Italy, the decisive concept of government was not the American but the French one – and not only because Italy stood under the protection of the bayonet of the Second Empire.

In *France*, the sceptics in the National Assembly of 1848 worked on the assumption that the 'doctrinaire pro-republicans' with their love of America were doomed, since they failed to see that France was not a federalist country.[8]

As far as the federal structure was concerned, the influence of the American model in those days was limited to *Switzerland* and Germany. Even Swiss constitutional lawyers, who were proud of their own federal tradition, worked on the assumption that the 'federal state was an American invention'.[9] What they meant was that America had made the transition from confederate to federal state before Switzerland.

'The heavy, unforgettable debt of Swiss public law' was, according to this point of view, only paid back, and then only in part, when 'several individual American states adopted the right of initiative and referendum along Swiss lines'.[10] The attention that each of the two federalist prototypes have paid to each other has by no means been equal. The Swiss have always studied the American model conscientiously and they have adapted a number of elements from it, whereas the Americans have tended to regard the Swiss model as anachronistic.[11]

The first imitation of a modern federal form of government was to be imposed on the Swiss from the outside. The Malmaison Draft Constitution of 1801, created by Napoleon and Talleyrand, bore striking resemblances to the American model, for instance in ascribing greater powers to the senate than to the lower house, in the Federal Diet and in the single-headed executive. The conclusion that these similarities were 'coincidental'[12] was based on the belief that Napoleon was not capable of undertaking a comparison with America. This draft never came into force and, for a long time, the basic concepts behind it played no part during the period of restoration after 1815 – a period that was characterized by cantonal particularism. It was not until the 1830s that the American model was brought into the debate again, by way of contrast to the confederate concept of Swiss federalism. The Lucerne Radical, Troxler argued in favour of the American model since 'the founding fathers of the North American Union States have resolved an inherent problem of humanity and, through their Union Constitution, have called into being the idea of a dynamic society, which, from now on in world history, must count as decisive for all federal republics.'[13]

In the meantime, the Civil War of 1847 had created the necessary political preconditions for the federal form and the bicameral system following the American pattern now represented the basis for a possible compromise between centralists and confederalists.[14] The strongest political grouping in Switzerland, the *Freisinnige* (Radical Liberals), would, in those days, also have liked to have a step towards the '*république une et indivisible*'. However, the resistance of the Catholic and French-speaking cantons as well as the risk of foreign intervention by the powers guaranteeing Swiss neutrality excluded that sort of option.[15]

Although the compromise of a bicameral system of American origin was very much in the air, according to the general tenor of contemporary press articles, there was still considerable resistance to this solution in 1848. The main arguments were the 'foreign origin' and 'extravagance and expense' of the system.[16] Rüttimann, a member of the Zurich Cantonal Council, who participated in these debates, was less than enthusiastic in a retrospective description of the mood behind the compromise:

> In 1848 the bicameral system appeared just as foreign to the Swiss as it is second nature for the Americans, and has been ever since the founding of

the Union. In Switzerland, this institution was regarded either as an aristocratic construction or as the fantasy of theoreticians with no practical experience, and we would never ever have had the idea of introducing it, had it not transpired to be the only means of finding an equitable settlement of the conflict between the interests and demands of the bigger and smaller cantons.[17]

All subsequent attempts to expand judicial review in the full American sense of the term were repeatedly blocked between 1912 and 1939 – with the reasoning that the sovereign Swiss people could counteract unpopular laws by means of a referendum and that this was the best guarantee for the Constitution.[18]

The Swiss Constitution of 1848 had only granted the Federal Court constitutional jurisdiction in those cases transferred to it by the legislator and virtually no case was ever referred to the Court for its judgement.

The parliament, which was elected by means of the majority principle and was dominated by the Radical liberals (*Freisinnige*), regarded constitutional jurisdiction as too much of a privilege to entrust it to a court which was strictly legalistic and hence impossible to control in political terms. In its explanatory statement on the complete revision of the Federal Constitution in 1870, the Federal Council (i.e. the government) was still using patronizing language in stating that the constitutional rights were still too ill-defined for a judge to be able to do anything with them.[19] This statement showed the difficulty that still existed in Europe in implementing the American idea of checks and balances in the face of the principles of popular sovereignty and the French revolution.

In *Germany*, in the course of the constitutional work in the *Paulskirche*, there were two further sources of resistance which did not exist in Switzerland. First of all, Germany was a federation of monarchies. There was none of that 'kindred republican spirit' which was portrayed as a bond between the USA and Switzerland. Here, it was not possible to propagate republicanism and federalism as two parts of one and the same whole as in Switzerland, since it was claimed that, in social terms, equality was a *sine qua non* for the liberal republic.

The constitutional committee of the German National Assembly in the *Paulskirche*, on the other hand, 'allowed itself to hope' (as its own timid wording put it) that similar effects would emerge from constitutional monarchy.[20]

In addition, there were member states (Austria being the prime example) which included large territories that were not regarded as part of the German Empire. The discussion in plenary hardly dealt with the principles of federalism and the existing examples thereof, it concentrated on the geographic extent of the applicability of the new system. What was most at issue were the partially non-German duchies of Schleswig and Posen, whose right to belong to the Empire seemed unclear. The majority of members of the constitutional committee did make references to both the American and Swiss models.[21] A radical minority point of view put forward by Robert Blum, Franz Wigard and Schüler included the desire to strengthen the centralist element in the draft, and wanted to go even further than the American model. The reason given was the USA's protected military position compared with that of a country in the middle of a continent, such as Germany:

> On the contrary, given Germany's external circumstances and the current balance of power, we regard a strong, rigid, indivisible union as being absolutely necessary. We find the essential reason for this not only in the fact that Germany is surrounded by powerful neighbours with unitary constitutions, with whom it is in constant close contact and with whom it could find itself involved in large-scale conflicts at virtually any time, and this would, therefore, also require the unification of all its forces in a single hand – a consideration which is of much less moment in the case of the United States of North America on account of that federal state's more isolated position.[22]

When later on in the post-1871 German Empire, federalism degenerated to pseudo-federalism, those defending the system used very cynical language on occasions in exploiting the comparison between Germany's insecure position and the secure position of the USA. To quote one of them, the historian, Treitschke:[23]

> They need have no fear of the Mexicans, that rotting Creole state; and as far as Canada is concerned, they have so little to worry them that they can rather think in strong terms of actually swallowing up that country themselves at some stage, and I would wish them the very best of luck in so doing.

Since only very incomplete and sketchy minutes of the constitutional committee have survived, the influence of the American model on the draft constitution of the German Empire can only be judged by comparing the actual texts. The effects of the American model were considerable, especially as regards the allocation of powers in the federal state and its financial constitution.[24] This constitution never gained any real significance but it is certainly an exaggeration when Friedrich concludes: 'Perhaps its very Americanism must be considered part of its failure.'[25]

The mood in the country was not hostile to adopting considerable portions from America, as is shown by the majority of pamphlets printed at the time. It was more the case that the monarchs resisted the erosion of their sovereignty and that the revolutionary pressure from the street had abated somewhat. Only a revolution, bringing with it a radical reform of the established states, could have made such a constitution viable.

Right into the twentieth century the prejudice persisted vigorously that federalism and parliamentary majority government could not be combined. This message was taken especially to heart in *Latin America*. The federal systems in Argentina, Brazil, Mexico and Venezuela combined the American model in both important elements. They followed the American arrangement of separation of powers, except that the competence of central government became much more comprehensive than in the USA.[26]

Given the constant stream of *coups d'etat* and changes in government, the Latin American constitutional development was not regarded as having any major educative value. To all intents and purposes, the American institutions remained foreign for a different type of cacique society. The blinkered European-centred view of things, however, prevented two excellently operational overseas systems from being used to prove the prejudices wrong, namely those of Australia and Canada. The extent of their independence has, however, been underestimated in Europe. It is only since Austria, after the First World War, and the Federal Republic of Germany, after the Second World War, have succeeded in combining parliamentary government with federalism that this prejudice has died out (the Weimar Republic was neither truly federal nor fully parliamentarian). It was by no means an easy task for Canada and Australia, in their turn, to graft American principles on to the British system of institutions.

In the case of *Canada* especially, the American model has repeatedly had attractive and repulsive effects at the same time.[27] No less an authority than the British constitutional lawyer, Dicey, popularized the theory that the British North America Act of 1867 had not come about without those responsible having 'the American Constitution constantly before their eyes', and had Canada been an independent country, then a constitution similar to that of the United States would certainly have emerged.[28]

Later research took a more subtle view of events. When the politicians met in Charlottetown and later in Quebec City they had indeed studied the US model with care. They deliberately chose not to accept the model, however, – not only on account of the presidential system but also because of federalism, since, for them, the Civil War appeared to be a delayed consequence of granting too much power to the individual states. Even the French-speaking Canadian representatives, who were far from happy with all the solutions, accepted many of the quasi-unitarian elements of the Canadian Constitution, which differed clearly from the federalism of the USA.[29]

Contemporaries, such as one of Nova Scotia's leading politicians, Joseph Howe, regarded the Canadian constitution as an unfortunate mixture of the British and the American models:

> We had two examples to guide us, that of England and that of the United States. The delegates offer us the constitution of neither. . . This hybrid resembles nothing on this continent, or on the other. The fare presented to us is neither fish, flesh, nor good red herring.[30]

It was not only in the concentration of powers that Canada remained closer to the motherland, the same applied to the whole constitutional concept. Apart from the British North America Act of 1867, a further seven Acts of Parliament were taken to make up 'Canada's Constitution' during the revision talks of 1964, and even in its 1982 version a single constitution has still not been moulded.[31]

Canada's constitutional development was much less uniform than were the compromises concluded in Australia in the 1890s and which, on the whole, have turned out to be durable, given the remarkable homogeneity of the Australian population. In Canada, on the other hand, the problems with Quebec and the West have thrown federalism into serious crises. In the reform process of the 1970s the American model was only rarely quoted, since it did not promise any solutions to Canada's problems. Despite the conflicts, the national self-awareness of the Canadian population has increased tremendously as a reaction to the growing American dominance of the USA in nearly all areas of Canadian life.[32]

The Western Provinces have hardly let their dissatisfaction with Ottawa grow into separatism and the idea of joining the USA as a separate state was only approved by 3 per cent of the population in 1980.[33] The old Canadian Constitution was classified as 'quasi-federal' (as opposed to the American or Swiss model) on account of the central government's powers to influence provincial legislation.[34] In addition, the Senate was never an effective platform for the interests of the Provinces – contrary to the role of the second chamber in other federal systems.[35] That is why the reform turned into primarily a reform of federalism:

> Our constitutional discussion has been about federalism; and federalism in Canada has been primarily about the balance between regional and national communities rather than about preserving democracy and rights.[36]

Nonetheless, the inclusion of a catalogue of basic human rights and the strengthening of the Supreme Court must lead us to view this statement in purely relative terms and the Canadian system has moved nearer to the American model, quite apart from the issue of federalist reform. In Canada there was, however, only subdued enthusiasm regarding the reform, since major problems remain unresolved. The amendment process became transparent and a purely Canadian affair. Many experts, however, saw new difficulties in the solution to the Quebec problem, which was patched together with undue haste. It turned out to be impossible to carry through any noteworthy reforms of electoral law (to facilitate the formation of coalition governments).[37]

The comparison with America after the reform often still had a satirical ring to it:

> A familiar and rueful Canadian joke holds that, while Canada had hoped to achieve a synthesis of British governance, French culture and American know-how, it has been left, instead, with the residue of British know-how, French governance, and American culture.[38]

Australia received its independence in constitutional matters earlier than Canada did, since the British North America Act of 1867 had not even made provision for an amendment procedure. In Australia, a constitution displaying strong American inspiration came into force in 1901. Other models were, however, also discussed. One member of the Sydney Convention complained:

> We have had the American Constitution and the Swiss Constitution, and slabs of the Canadian Constitution hurled at us from all sides *ad nauseam*. We have had nothing else but this American Constitution from all sides of the House, and to bolster up every kind of opinion, and I have come to the conclusion that the American Constitution is such a many-sided one that it can be used to back up every argument on every possible side of the federation question.[39]

In Australia it was thus also a frequent complaint that the American model was being put to use in party struggles. Here again, it was less a question of implementing a much-admired model than of reinforcing a particular line of argument. Since, as one of the American founding fathers put it, a constitution ought to be 'short and obscure', then the American Constitution was better suited for a politicized debate, since it appeared to be shorter, more obscure and in greater need of interpretation when compared with later constitutions. However, this interpretation was not really one which the Australians arrived at directly. In this area as well as in others, interpretation still required the services of arbitrators back in the metropolitan countries. In this particular case, the choice fell primarily on Lord Bryce's authoritative British interpretation of America. The Canadian influence was less, since Canadian federalism and other provisions of the British North America Act were regarded as not going far enough.[40]

The relations of the peripheral countries with one another have remained underdeveloped even today. Intellectual ties were no less strongly organized via the metropolitan states than economic ones. In Australia it was possible to have a free and exhaustive discussion on the alternatives of presidential and parliamentary government. A not inconsiderable number of Australians were in favour of the American or Swiss model as a means of securing federalism.

John Cockburn wrote the following passage in 1890:

> We do not know that the responsibility of ministers to parliament can exist under any other conditions. We have not seen it exist in the United States or in Switzerland, and we have no reason to suppose that it will be compatible with conditions of federation here.[41]

At the Adelaide Convention in 1987, Dobson and others renewed the arguments in favour of a dualist system. It was only the Labour Party that was in favour of stronger centralization and would have preferred an adaptation of the Canadian model rather than the American one.[42]

After the First World War, the establishment of the *Soviet Union* created the first-ever Socialist federal state. America as a model was evoked in the course of the discussions – but mainly for the purposes of demarcation. Federalism as such was not regarded as more liberal than the unitarian state and Marx's opinion that federalism could only be recommended where different peoples were present in a single state tended to prevail. That is why Marx and Engels rejected federalism in Germany. Federalism made its way into the Soviet Constitution not because of any fundamental theoretical considerations but out of practical necessity. As the principle of the shape of the structure of a state (*gosudarstvennoe ustroistvo*) it was regarded as less significant than the political regime (*politicheskii rezhim*) determined by class structure. That explains why the Soviet federation was regarded as being incomparably more progressive than the American one. In many places, Soviet literature admits that pre-1917 bolshevism had anti-federalist leanings.[43]

The American model was dismissed with expressions such as 'a petty-bourgeois anarchistic Babitt ideal of federalism'.[44] It was called petty bourgeois because it was based on a static non-historical ideal of federalism, laid down as dogma once and for all.[45] This clear demarcation vis-à-vis America did not, however, exclude the occasional point of inspiration from the American model.

After the Second World War, *Yugoslavia* became the second Socialist state to implement a federalist system. In the meantime it has gone far beyond the Soviet model and has developed into authentic federalism, especially since only one of the two centralizing clamps in Socialism (i.e. the party – the other being centralized planning) has remained since 1965. The first Constitution of 1945 was, broadly speaking, a copy of the Soviet one of 1936. There are virtually no signs of American influences.[46] It was only later that political writers in Yugoslavia began to take a genuine interest in the American doctrine[47] for the purposes of further developing their country's own federalism – something which had become necessary in the light of the growing centrifugal tendencies in the six republics and the two autonomous regions.

The most direct influence of the American model on the structure of federalism appeared to be on the defeated powers after 1945. In the case of *Japan*, they renounced the grafting on of an artificial federalism. In *Germany*, the emphasis on federalism amounted to preaching to the converted. Constitutional writers in that country were more or less unanimous in trying to establish links with the German federal tradition that went back to the Middle Ages until the period before 1866 when Bismarck increasingly set about demolishing it. Allied intervention in the constituent process in Germany was concerned with federalism more than anything else. The American 'grants-in-aid' system was probably advocated less because of a doctrinaire belief in the superiority of their own system than because of a lack of knowledge of or confidence in other systems. Even in the area of federalism, the Allies let astonishing details go through, such as the bureaucratic, non-representative *Bundesrat* (Federal Council), with the remark that such a construction would give the *Länder* (German states) a greater say in national decisions than the American Senate.[48]

The adoption of the American model of the Senate, which is what the SPD wanted, failed on account of resistance from Adenauer and large sections of the CDU. Süsterhenn, a CDU member, deliberately opted against the American model and for the German constitutional tradition:

> It is both possible and correct to refer to the example of the United States of North America and Switzerland, where federal forms of state exist without a federal council and merely with a senate elected at state level. I am, however, of the opinion that it would be more correct if we Germans were to continue our own national tradition and to decide in favour of a system that is after all rooted in German constitutional history and has proven itself beyond challenge.[49]

The SPD advocated the American model of a senate not so much on the basis of enthusiasm for America but more for party political reasons, since its power base was concentrated more in the smaller city states and it was thus able to calculate that it would stand to gain from the equal representation of the American-type Senate. The pretext that this principle was more democratic was attacked in many ways. Theodor Heuss (FDP), later to become the first Federal President, said the following in addressing the main committee:

> The reference to foreign examples is inaccurate, since both in Switzerland and in America the federal state was built up by smallish regions which were all rather similar. There were no really major differences between the American States in 1776.[50]

He forgot to add that, given the tremendous differences in population between New York and Nevada, equality of representation in the Senate would presumably no longer have been so easy to implement in the twentieth century as *the* democratic solution. Since Calhoun, the deviation from the numeric majority as a principle of democracy has also been repeatedly justified in America with a doctrine of 'concurrent majorities'.

Taking *India* as an example, it became obvious that America was often able to serve as a pattern for the structure of institutions. The actual reason was to be found more in a particular tendency in the former British colonies, which led to a parallel development to that in the USA. The British policy of '*divide and rule*' led, in a period of gradual decolonization, to different British colonies coming together to form a federal state. Federalism (an idea foreign to the British concept of government) was adopted as a compromise to prevent government anarchy in the post-colonial status. India is a case which differed from the examples of Australia and Canada insofar as what occurred was '*devolution*', whereby a federal state developed out of what had been a centralized colonial *raj*.[51]

Once the major phases of the constitution of new states had been concluded the influence of the American model could be detected more in the way American processes were dealt with in the world's various federal states. There can be no doubt that America has taken on a leadership role here and, thanks to having the world's most developed political science it has also become the pace-setter for coining terms and the theoretical appraisal of the processes within federal states. By comparison, Switzerland, the second big model, has become very much overshadowed. The tendency has been for Switzerland to follow what was happening in the Federal Republic of Germany rather than for borrowings in the opposite direction to seem more feasible.

In most of the federations, increasing modernization, nationwide communications and mobility have led to a process of centralization. Increasing centrifugal tendencies have only become apparent in multi-ethnic federations such as Canada and Yugoslavia. Comparatively speaking, Australia and Switzerland have maintained the balance between the various levels better than the USA or the Federal Republic of Germany. The theory of *cooperative federalism* (with its forms of horizontal cooperation between states) and that of intergovernmental policy-making with the horizontal cooperation of federal and state bureaucracies has been most strongly adopted in the Federal Republic of Germany.[53] The development of federal states and the degree to which development trends in America could be imitated depended *inter alia* on the party system. Despite the two-party system, the USA was one of those federations where the strong local roots of the party system had the effect of limiting the integrating force of the political parties. In Canada, regional fragmentation is even greater still. Australia is somewhere between the two. This type may be contrasted with the consociational democracies where strategies aimed at consensus and proportional arrangements lead to a broad measure of agreement between the federal and state levels, as in Austria and Switzerland.

Somewhere between these two models we find the Federal Republic of Germany, where, particularly during the period of SPD government, certain frictions have been detected between the federal and the state level.[54] Despite this particular divergence compared with the USA, the developments in the German federal state have most closely paralleled those in the United States.

Notes

1   William H. Riker: *Federalism. Origin, Operation, Significance*, Boston, Little Brown, 1964, pp. 8ff.
2   Kenneth C. Wheare: *Federal Government*, London, Oxford UP, 1963, 4th edn. p. 1.
3   Carl J. Friedrich: *The Impact of American Constitutionalism abroad*, Boston, Boston UP, 1967, p. 43.
4   Max von Seydel: *Staatsrechtliche und politische Abhandlungen*, Freiburg, 1893, p. 87.
5   Luis Loureiro Junior: *Parlamentarismo e presidencialismo*, Sao Paulo, 1962, pp. 163ff.
6   Robert R. Bowie/Carl J. Friedrich (eds.): *Studies in Federalism*, Boston, Little Brown, 1954, p. 84.
7   Gabriela Rosa: *Genesi e sviluppo degli S.U.d'A.. Commentari dell'Ateno di Brescia*, 1880, p. 179.
8   Eugene Newton Curtis: *The French Assembly of 1848 and American Constitutional Doctrines*, New York. Columbia University. PhD thesis, 1917, p. 228.
9   Eduard His: *Amerikanische Einflüsse im schweizerischen Verfassungsrecht*, in: Festgabe der Basler Juristenfakultäten und des Basler Juristenvereins zum Schweizerischen Juristentag. Basle, Helbing & Lichtenhahn, 1920, (81-110), p. 82.
10   Myron Luehrs Tripp: *Der schweizerische und der amerikanische Bundesstaat*, Zurich, Polygraphischer Verlag, 1942, p. 1.
11   Francois Da Pozzo: *Die Schweiz in der Sicht des Auslandes*, Berne, Francke, 1977, pp. 123ff.

12   Luehrs Tripp, op. cit. p. 9.

13   Ignaz Paul Vital Troxler: *Die Verfassung der Vereinigten Staaten Nordamerikas als Musterbild der schweizerischen Bundesreform*, Schaffhausen, Brodtmann, 1848, p. 11.

14   Eduard His: *Geschichte des neuen Schweizerischen Staatsrechts*, Vol. 1. *Der Bundesstaat von 1848 bis 1914*. Basle, Helbing & Lichtenhahn, 1938, 1st Half-Volume, p. 357.

15   William E. Rappard: *La constitution fédérale de la Suisse. 1848-1948*, Neuchâtel, La Baconnière, 1948, p. 118f.

16   Jürg Düblin: *Die Anfänge der Schweizerischen Bundesversammlung*, Berne. Francke, 1978, p. 17.

17   J. Rüttimann: Das nordamerikanische Bundesstaatsrecht verglichen mit den politischen Einrichtungen der Schweiz. Zurich, Orell, Füssli & Co., I. Theil, 1867, p. 118.

18   W.J. Wagner: *The Federal States and their Judiciary*, The Hague, Mouton, 1959, pp. 105ff.

19   Jörg P. Müller: in: *Die Verfassungsgerichtsbarkeit im Gefüge der Staatsfunktionen*. VVDStRL 39, Berlin, 1981, p. 58f.

20   Franz Wigard (ed.): *Stenographischer Bericht über die Verhandlungen der deutschen constituirenden Nationalversammlung zu Frankfurt am Main, 1848*, Vol. 4, p. 2724, col. 2.

21   Wigard, op. cit., Vol. 4, p. 2723, col. 2.

22   Wigard, op. cit., Vol. 4, p. 2742, col. 2, p. 2743, col. 1.

23   Heinrich von Treitschke: *Politik*, Leipzig, Hirzel, 1898, Vol. 2, p. 276.

24   Anton Scholl: *Einfluss der nordamerikanischen Unionsverfassung auf die Verfassung des Deutschen Reiches vom 28. März 1849*, thesis, Tübingen, 1913, pp. 47ff.

25   Friedrich, op. cit., 1967, p. 54.

26   William S. Stokes: *Latin American Politics*, New York, Crowell, 1959, p. 485.

27   Alexander Brady: *Democracy in the Dominions*, Toronto UP, 1947, 1958, p. 39.

28   A.V. Dicey: *Law of the Constitution*, London, Macmillan, (1885) 1962, p. 166.

29   Donald S. Smiley: *Canada in Question: Federalism in the Eighties*, Toronto, McGraw-Hill Ryerson, 1980, 3rd Edn., p. 10.

30   cited in: J. Murray Beck: *Joseph Howe: Voice of Nova Scotia*, Toronto, McClelland & Stewart, 1964, pp. 173f.

31   cf Smiley, op. cit., p. 17.

32   Garth Stevenson: *Unfulfilled Union. Canadian Federalism and National Unity*, Toronto, Gage, 1982, pp. 76f.

33   Ronald James Zukowsky: *Struggle over the Constitution. From the Quebec Referendum to the Supreme Court*, Kingston/Ontario. Institute of Intergovernmental Relations. 1981, p. 133.

34   Wheare, op. cit. p. 18.

35   Stanley M. Beck/Ivan Bernier (eds.): *Canada and the New Constitution*, Montreal, Institute for Research on Public Policy, 1983, Vol. 1, p. 43.

36   Keith Banting/Richard Simeon; *And No One Cheered. Federalism, Democracy and the Constitution Act*, Toronto, Methuen, 1983, p. 355.

37   Banting/Simeon, op. cit., p. 93; Ronald G. Landes: *The Canadian Polity. A Comparative Introduction*, Scarborough, Prentice-Hall Canada 1983, pp. 417ff; Beck/Bernier, op. cit., Vol. 1, pp. 55ff.

38   Edgar Z. Friedenberg: *Defence to Authority: The Case of Canada*, White Plains, Sharpe, 1980, p. 107.

39   Erling M. Hunt: *American Precedents in Australian Federation*, New York, Columbia UP, 1930, p.136.

40   Alexander Brady: *Democracy in the Dominions. A Comparative Study in Institutions*, Toronto UP, 1947, 1955, p. 153.
41   John A. Cockburn: *Australian Federation*, London, Horace Marshall 1901, p. 139.
42   L.F. Crisp: *Australian National Government*, London, Longmans, 1965, p. 28.
43   D.L. Zlatopolski: *Obrazovanie i razvitie SSSR kak soyuznogo gosudarstva*, Moscow, Jurlit, 1954, p. 15.
44   Idem p. 11.
45   cf Klaus von Beyme: *Der Föderalismus in der Sowjetunion*, Heidelberg, Quelle & Meyer, 1964, pp. 38ff.
46   Robert K. Furtak: *Jugoslawien. Politik, Gesellschaft, Wirtschaft*, Hamburg, Hoffmann & Campe, 1975, p. 50.
47   cf Vojslav Stanovcič (ed.): *Federalistički spisi*, Belgrade, Ranička stampa, 1981, pp. 18ff.
48   Peter H. Merkl: *Die Entstehung der Bundesrepublik Deutschland*, Stuttgart, Kohlhammer, 1968, 2nd edn., p. 133.
49   Parlamentarischer Rat. Stenographische Berichte über die Plenarsitzungen. Bonn 1948/49, p. 24, col. 2.
50   *Parlamentarischer Rat: Verhandlungen des Hauptausschusses*, Bonn 1948/49, p. 126, col. 2.
51   Günther Doeker: *Parlamentarische Bundesstaaten im Commonwealth of Nations: Kanada, Australien, Indien*, Tübingen, Mohr, 1980, Vol. 1, p. 9.
52   Da Pozzo, op. cit. p. 126.
53   cf. Klaus von Beyme: West Germany: Federalism, in: *International Political Science Review*, 1984, No. 4, pp. 381-396.
54   On the three types: Klaus von Beyme: *Political Parties in Western Democracies*, New York, St. Martins, 1985, pp. 217ff.

4 Judicial Review

The principle of judicial review of laws and other legal provisions was once referred to as 'America's most important export'.[1]

This principle was often seen as the corollary of the dualist presidential system, since it is possible for that form of dualism to lead to much more serious conflicts than the unified decision-making body in parliamentary majority government. In addition, the principle of judicial review has been regarded as a necessity in federal states. Wheare has assessed the principle as an essential criterion of federalism, alongside the supremacy of the constitution and a difficult amendment procedure.[2]

The first of these two linkages does not necessarily have to be the case. Today more parliamentary systems than presidential ones have established a variation on the theme of constitutional jurisdiction. Federative states (with the exception of the Soviet Union, which, being a Socialist state believes, unlike Yugoslavia, that it does not need any constitutional jurisdiction[3]) have otherwise all adopted this institution. In the meantime, however, sufficient unitarian states have also introduced constitutional jurisdiction. This has even occurred in France – but in a watered-down form. Resistance to this institution was strongest in this country on account of the doctrine of the sovereignty of the people. This French doctrine and the British theory of the sovereignty of parliament were the strongest barriers to the concept of the supremacy of the constitution out of which constitutional jurisdiction evolved.

Following the Second World War many European sceptics felt they were justified in their prejudice against the principle of judicial review since the three losing powers, Germany, Italy and Japan, adopted this principle – it being frequently wrongly assumed (except in the case of Japan) that it was imposed upon them.[4]

In Germany, a number of well-known constitutional lawyers also overlooked the roots of this institution in all the states that had formerly belonged to the German Empire. In a speech delivered in 1962, Rudolph Smend described the Federal Constitutional Court (*Bundesverfassungsgericht*) as a 'green-house plant'; it had 'not grown in the open air of a sovereign state and people but had been influenced, and even protected, by the occupying powers'.[5]

In Roman law countries, the prejudice persisted for a long time that constitutional jurisdiction was only meaningful in a *common law* tradition. America, in particular, demonstrated that its rigid constitution was compatible with common law traditions. America was able to become the pioneer of judicial review because it was also the pioneer of modern constitutionalism, where the idea of the supremacy of the constitution played an important role – not only in the protection of federalism. Where the sovereignty of parliament was the basis of the *raison d'état* as in Great Britain, constitutional jurisdiction could only develop in a rudimentary form (for instance the impeachment of ministers in the Upper House). Where the idea of the sovereignty of the people went so far in practice as to allow for legislation by referendum, as in Switzerland, there was also resistance to constitutional jurisdiction.

In the nineteenth century there were four main areas where constitutional jurisdiction developed more than anywhere else:[6]

1   In decisions regarding *constitutional conflicts* between individual states. Constitutional jurisdiction developed as a purely federal institution in Switzerland, where the Federal Court offers protection of the individual's constitutional rights only vis-à-vis the cantonal authorities. The extension of this principle to federal acts would have appeared as an affront to the sovereignty of the people in the eyes of the Radical Liberals (*Freisinnige*) who were the main political force behind the 1848 constitution.[7]

2   The judicial review of acts and international treaties was only implemented after the First World War and had only been demanded on isolated occasions in previous writings. On this occasion, it was Austria that pioneered the development.

3   The protection of constitutionally guaranteed rights of individuals (the challenge of a law's constitutionality). There had

been earlier, less developed forms of this in the right of appeal to the German *Reichskammergericht* and a limited variation on the same theme is mentioned above in the provision applicable in Switzerland since 1848.

4   Procedures for groups or individuals to seek to protect constitutions for preventive or repressive reasons. The impeachment of ministers was a common form in the nineteenth century and appeared to be compatible even with the British principle of the sovereignty of Parliament, especially since it was the Upper House that had to take the decision on impeachment. This form became generally obsolete as a result of the political responsibility of ministers before Parliament, despite which, provisions regarding the impeachment of ministers or the President have been retained in several constitutions.

The differences in the areas needing measures placed narrow limits on the adoption of the American model, because it always needed to be adjusted to individual legal traditions. It was also an area which could not simply be read off straight out of the American Constitution. Those interested in adopting it were thus forced to acquaint themselves with the actual developments since the 1803 judgment in *Marbury versus Madison*. Writing in the *Federalist Papers*, Hamilton had still maintained:

> The judiciary on the contrary, has no influence over either the sword or the purse; no direction either of the strength or the wealth of the society; and can take no active resolution whatever. It may truly be said to have neither force nor will but merely judgment and must ultimately depend on the aid of the executive arm even for the efficacy of its judgments.[8]

In questions of foreign policy this statement was broadly correct but in questions of the economy and society, on the other hand, there were much more far-reaching cases of judicial intervention than envisaged by the founding fathers. Judicial review could only be developed by the gradual disappearance of the passive view of judges merely applying the law.

European legal tradition took a different course from the American model early on through its tendency to develop a system of highly specialized courts, which to the American view of liberty would have seemed like tyrannical feudal law or a star chamber procedure. The American Supreme Court and the highest courts of the federal states are not constitutional courts but the highest instance of the normal judicial procedure. A case may be referred to one of these courts by means of a normal appeal; a special procedure is not necessary, as in the Austrian model of 1920, which had a strong influence on Italy and the Federal Republic of Germany and later also on Spain. The separation of constitutional jurisdiction has been defended by continental lawyers with reference to legal tradition and the sociological position of judges: European judge is, they claim, used to a hermeneutic technique, avoiding policy making-type decisions. According to Calamandrei, constitutional jurisdiction must contain 'polemic against the past and a reform programme for the future' or, as the President of the Austrian Constitutional Court, Walter Antoniolli, once put it: 'Something more is demanded of the Constitutional Court, namely a legislative act to correct the Legislator'.[9]

It was thus considered that the implementation of constitutional provisions was an activity for which the professional judges were not, as a rule, prepared.[10] The frequently mistrusted manner of their appointment by the legislature was also justified in terms of the particular political and social demands placed on judges.

It was only in German-speaking areas (in states which had once belonged to the German Empire) that there was a tradition which seemed to favour the emergence of constitutional jurisdiction *ab initio*. In the German Confederation (1815–1866) the setting up of such an institution failed on account of opposition from the Southern German states. Memories of the *Reichskammergericht* and the *Reichshofrat* (belittled by the Prussian view of German history, which excluded Austria) were still kept alive in frequent political publications.

In the *Paulskirche* a large-scale adoption of the American model did finally emerge. In no other single question was the USA so frequently brought into the debate.[11] There was resistance in Germany as well. Members of the Constitutional Committee expressed their objections to proceedings against infringements of basic rights. Representations to parliament and the government seemed to many critics to fit in with the system better. Even among those who accepted the *principle* of constitutional jurisdiction, there were disagreements as to who should have the right to initiate proceedings. The Heidelberg lawyer, Mittermaier settled the dispute with his claim that:

> We must choose between two systems: the Swiss have made the assumption that such a case (of states always going directly to the imperial court over the head of the imperial government) could not be accepted at all. . . In America they have precisely the opposite system; there it is the national court itself that has the sole right to decide on its powers.[12]

In the plenary debate, Moriz Mohl of Stuttgart expressed his doubt about demanding too much of the Imperial Court in resolving issues of political controversy. His line of argument brought out differences between Germany and America, which were seen above all in the federation of monarchies:

> To the best of my knowledge, it is only in North America that a court has been set up, before which the central authority must establish or accept rights vis-à-vis the individual states. But, Gentlemen, there are not 34 princes in North America. In North America, the central authority has the people as a whole as its only counterpart and the people does not have the same interest that the monarchist German governments might think they have, namely, of working against the central authority, since the people knows full well that its interest is represented by the central authority and its representatives in presidential parliament; the people will thus not rise up against its own representatives without due cause. In Germany, where we *do* experience the daily disobedience of the governments vis-à-vis the central authority, the governments are often likely to have the idea of initiating proceedings regarding the powers of the central authority and of Parliament. . .[13]

In putting this case, he exaggerated the unity of republican member states in the American Union, but it probably remains true that the German princes, who had decided in favour of the confederation largely under pressure, would have used such an instrument to develop even greater obstructionist desires against the central authority. The never-ending cases of litigation in the old German Empire were still felt in the bones of learned students of legal history.

The Heidelberg professor, Mittermaier, a member of the Committee of Three, which had a key influence on the draft under debate, gave a truly authoritative lecture on the American Supreme Court. He also took a stance against the advocates of the sovereignty of parliament, making reference to Tocqueville in the French National Assembly, when the latter tried to dispel the old prejudice regarding decisions on political questions being taken in the courts: 'Gentlemen! It is not true that the highest court in America takes the principal decision on the political issues in all political cases.'[14]

The debate drifted into a series of quotations and counter-quotations, when, in answering Robert Mohl, he concluded with a *captatio benevolentiae* in favour of the American model:

> To the best of my knowledge, the Imperial Minister will, himself, agree with these ideas, since they were already sketched out in his classical book on America. Gentlemen! Let us have a full discussion on the necessary addition to the court in the light of American experience; I urge you, Gentlemen, to give the Constitution this keystone, a keystone which guarantees freedom, and one that gives every individual citizen the possi-

bility of securing justice against the highest and against the most lowly; a keystone which will make possible the German unity which is otherwise on very shaky ground.[15]

The applause, however, came only from the Left.

The Imperial Constitutional Court (*Reichsgericht*) of the *Paulskirche* Constitution was the first case of specialized constitutional jurisdiction in Europe. It was not a court of appeal (along the lines of the French Revolution) nor the highest level of appeal above the courts of the individual states, it was a genuine constitutional court (or rather a *Staatsgerichtshof* ['government tribunal'] in the parlance of the time). It was the right to challenge constitutionality provided for in Paragraph 126 that was designed to give the comprehensive catalogue of basic rights its full enforcement.

The powers of the Imperial Court went beyond those in Switzerland in that the Imperial institutions were also subject to its jurisdiction. As regards other characteristics it tended more to resemble the Swiss solution: it was the federal guarantee that was at the centre of its conception, not the judicial review of legal acts, which distinguished it from the later Austro-German model.[16] Even American observers were impressed. The American historian, George Bancroft, who was envoy in London at the time (and who was otherwise exceptionally taken with American achievements) praised the Imperial Court: 'it is a great improvement on our own, the best thing in the world; Germany for ever'.[17]

In the second half of the century the American principle of judicial review was particularly influential in the British dominions; the adoption of federalism had also set the course towards constitutional jurisdiction. The British North America act of 1867 did not yet provide for judicial review in *Canada*. In 1875, a Supreme Court was nonetheless set up by ordinary statute. Despite the inspiration drawn from the US model, the judges hardly carved out a profile for themselves in the political process in line with the American example. They carry out a very restricted judicial review of legal acts, and under the new constitution of 1982 (which does, after all, incorporate a catalogue of basic rights) the prospects for a comprehensive defence of basic rights, such as exists in America, are rather limited.[18]

The inclusion of a 'Charter of Rights' is a much delayed imitation of the American example which, contrary to the French model, inserted the catalogue of basic rights later in the form of the First Amendments. This step signifies a radical break with constitutional tradition, which was aimed at 'continuity and incremental development' and was regarded in many quarters as placing too great a burden on the courts, which had not been prepared for the new tasks.[19]

In *Australia* the legal system was somewhat less strongly influenced by America than was federalism. Here, a number of elements were also adopted from the Canadian system.[20]

It is not only in the institutional specialization but also in the underlying concepts that constitutional jurisdiction in Europe has moved further and further away from the American model. The American model has been called a *'diffuse judicial review of acts'*.[21] In the *Austrian* model, on the other hand, *'concentrated judicial review of acts'* was implemented for the first time. On the basis of pure legal doctrine, Hans Kelsen used his influence as the special adviser to Karl Renner, the State Chancellor of the provisional Germano-Austrian government, to promote the constitutional court. Later on he often referred to it as 'his favourite child'. The passages he had drafted on the constitutional court made their way into the constitution with only insignificant amendments. There is little evidence that Kelsen had the American example in mind at the time.[22] In the commentaries on Kelsen's *Collection of Austrian Constitutional Laws*, it is even stated explicitly: 'In all the drafts, the Swiss Constitution served as an example, alongside the Imperial German one.'[23]

Kelsen built on the tradition of the Imperial Court, which he developed further into a genuine constitutional court. Students of Kelsen waxed particularly lyrical in evidencing the Austrian origins of the idea:

> The fact that pure legal doctrine and constitutional jurisdiction as its practical manifestation, should have grown up on the soil of Greater Austria strikes us as no coincidence. The innumerable political disagreements between individual members of the Danube Empire as well as between members and the central authority have, since time immemorial, only rarely been fought out in armed struggles and, as a rule, have taken the form of legal disputes using arguments of constitutional law. If we bear in mind that Austria was the 'final political form of the old Roman Empire' then it does not seem exaggerated to claim that there is hardly any corner of the globe where the law and its strictest form is taken as seriously as in Vienna, the cradle of the Viennese school of legal history with its worldwide application in general and 'pure legal doctrine' in particular.[24]

Such self-glorification by the Kelsen school also came in for criticism in Austria itself and here we can refer to the long tradition of German constitutional lawyers from Mohl through to Jellinek who had expressed their views on the concept of constitutional jurisdiction before Kelsen, and also to the Austrian tradition, where in the more strongly federalist plans for restructuring the Empire the principle of judicial review cropped up time and again. Of these endeavours it was said: 'The American model had not been able to gain acceptance; but without the intellectual spur it provided, judicial review of laws would indeed not have reached the stage of positive acceptance so quickly'.[25]

A whole series of preconditions was needed to accelerate this positive acceptance. Perhaps part of the credit may also be ascribed to the American model itself, but political circumstances played a more important part in bringing about this breakthrough for judicial review. They included the state of latent civil war, a state which the majority did not want but which, nonetheless, had to come into being, since the Allies had forbidden annexation to the German Empire. Thus constitutional jurisdiction arose out of completely different sources from the American principle of judicial review. It came into being on account of the distrust in the various political camps. The state of tension called for stress-relieving institutions to be as apolitical as possible. It was not the federalist confict, as in the former Austria, but rather the ideological party political conflict which, by way of contrast to America, gave birth to the model. In discussing this solution, use was made of the term: 'a depersonalized substitute Emperor organized on a collegial basis'.[26]

The strong institutional safeguards for the Austrian Constitutional Court were a reflection of both old German legal traditions and new political necessities. The American model would have contributed to uncertainty in Europe, where the principle of *stare decisis* dominated (i.e. the lower courts are bound to the decisions of the highest court), which was not the case in common law countries. Some judges would regard a given legal provision as unconstitutional, whereas others would apply it. Even one and the same court could change its mind on a particular point over time. Given that a law, even after having been declared unconstitutional, would still remain in force, then, without the principle of *stare decisis*, the consequence would be that in every similar case it would be necessary to go through the courts again.

Switzerland found a middle course between the two models (the Austrian and the American ones) by giving the Federal court powers to decide beyond the particular concrete case and to render the law inoperable with an *erga omnes* effect.[27]

After the Second World War the Austrian model was adopted elsewhere in Europe, especially in Italy and the Federal Republic of Germany.

In *Italy*, the adoption of the principle was half-hearted and limited. Since Italy was not a federal state, the institution appeared superfluous to a large number of critics. It was, however, often justified with the argument that, contrary to the flexible *Statuto Albertino*, which could be amended by a simple decision of parliament along British lines, a rigid constitution with a difficult amendment procedure had now been created. Judicial review was hence recommended as a means of facilitating constitutional evolution. Even after its inclusion in the Constitution, the institution remained so controversial and foreign that it took seven years for parliament to pass the necessary legislation so that the *corte costituzionale* could begin its work.

In 1949, the *Federal Republic of Germany* tried to implement constitutional jurisdiction in its 'purest form'. The Federal Constitutional Court became a 'perfected Supreme Court'.[28] It was not a case of imposition by the occupying powers, as was sometimes postulated by political writers opposed to it. In the Allies' 'Frankfurt documents' of 1 July 1948, what was demanded was a 'federalist-type democratic constitution'. No attempt was made to urge the German constituents to accept constitutional jurisdiction. Nonetheless, the Supreme Court served as a model in many ways. The inclusion of this institution meant, however, that the Allies were more favourably inclined towards the German proposals (contrary to events in Japan). There is, on the other hand, virtually no evidence for Ridder's theory that the Allies renounced a right of veto because of constitutional jurisdiction.[29]

It was especially over the question of the appointment of judges that individual members of the Parliamentary Council such as the Chairman of the Main Committee, Carlo Schmid, were happy to make a point of emphasizing the political function of the new institution but, on the whole, the intention was to create something less of a politically influential body. Despite the long-standing German tradition of state jurisdiction (*'Staatsgerichtsbarkeit'*), there was also a great deal of uncertainty surrounding the new institution. Süsterhenn, a member of the Parliamentary Council, commented in the following terms when addressing that body: 'We are not afraid of the so-called justice-shaped politics as conjured up by Carlo Schmid's namesake with two "t"s'. He also made reference to the American example, where the Supreme Court had become the 'embodiment of the conscience of the whole people'.[30]

Those politicians who were apparently not entirely convinced of the new institution also fell victim to the suspicion that they were concurring with Carl Schmitt's discrimination against constitutional jurisdiction by dichotomizing between totalitarian and pluralist states – something Kelsen had campaigned against in the early 1930s.[31] It is, nevertheless, the considered view that the classical debate between Carl Schmitt and Hans Kelsen had no major influence on the fathers of the Constitution.[32]

Both protagonists had a clearer view of the political function of such an institution than did most of the draftsmen who elaborated the Basic Law. In addressing the Association of German Professors of Constitutional Law in 1929, Kelsen had pleaded in favour of 'excluding party-political influences' and recommended that the quashing of a statute through constitutional law should not have any retroactive effect.[33]

In the Parliamentary Council of 1948/49 the American model was repeatedly evoked by many of the principal speakers from Carlo Schmid to Walter Strauss, who later became a judge at the European Communities' Court of Justice in Luxemburg and a Secretary of State. In a memorandum, the latter made extensive references to the Supreme Court, and through this voluntary preliminary work he had acquainted himself so thoroughly in comparative terms that he was able to cope with most of the surprisingly sparse debate on this important point.

In his appeal for a single supreme court he cited primarily America but also the German legal tradition. The Americans were suspicious of special courts. It was only in Europe that the state refused to be treated on the same level as its citizens. He did, however, make an exception of 'purely political disputes', since '. . . contrary to the United States, the authority of a court made up solely of professional judges is not yet sufficient for such a task'.[34] He wanted to keep the German 'Supreme Court' out of political disputes, which is why constitutional disagreements were still to be referred to a special constitutional court.

In spite of such detailed explanations given by individual members of the Parliamentary Council, knowledge of America was, on the whole, limited. Given the Americans' insistence on speed, an initiation to comparative law (as has been usual in some of the sub-committees in France and Italy) was not possible in Germany. Many of the fathers of the constitution were less motivated by the American model and more by reaction to the injustice of the Nazi state and the deliberate renewal of ties with older constitutional traditions before the Bismarck era. Questions of principle regarding constitutional jurisdiction were dealt with in a surprisingly summary fashion. The delegations of the German states (*Länder*) who attended the Constitutional Committee in Herrenchiemsee in August 1948 on the invitation of the Bavarian Minister President, Hans Ehard, had done very little concrete preliminary work (with the exception of Bavaria itself). The working papers submitted by the state government of Bavaria came from the private sources of professors of constitutional law such as Hans Nawiasky (the creator of the Bavarian Constitution) and Hans Kelsen (the father of the Austrian Constitutional Court).[35]

To begin with, the question as to whether to create a special Constitutional Court or a single top court along the lines of the Supreme Court in the USA or in Switzerland was a completely open issue. It was the Parliamentary Council's sub-committee on the administration of justice that first settled the matter. When it came to agreeing on powers the Parliamentary Council adopted the proposals of the Herrenchiemsee meeting with surprisingly little disagreement.

In settling the details of constitutional jurisdiction, the Austrian model (the only existing example of its implementation within a European legal tradition) played an important part. Both Italy and the

Federal Republic of Germany were guided by it, not least because of the major influence of Nawiasky, who had studied under Kelsen. In individual areas of adoption in both Italy and the Federal Republic of Germany, there was, however, a move back towards the American model: in the three European countries it is not all the judges that exercise judicial review of acts themselves as in America. That is a matter for the constitutional court. Both systems adopted by the two defeated powers of the Second World War have once again moved back towards the American model, insofar as (contrary to Austria) all judges are empowered to refer any legislation they think might be unconstitutional for examination by the constitutional court. In another area, however, the two systems were, again, closer to the Austrian one: other bodies, and not only the courts, may appeal *principaliter* and not only *incidenter* to the Constitutional Court (i.e. on the basis of a concrete case). In Germany the right to file cases is even greater than in Italy, in fact, it extends down to the individual citizen who feels his basic rights have been violated. The willingness to defend democracy, strengthened by American encouragement and pressure, thus frequently had the effect of making it necessary to depart from that selfsame American model over individual points. The introduction of abstract judicial review of acts (which by no means everybody has come to accept as a felicitous solution) represents a further step away from the American model, its purpose being to grant as comprehensive a degree of legal protection as possible and not one restricted to the concrete issues of court cases. In this way, it is precisely the shortcomings of the American model that it has proved possible to avoid (something the Japanese copy apparently has not managed to do), where the incidental nature of judicial review of acts had the effect of excluding a judicial review of a *prima facie* unconstitutional statute.[36]

In this way, the European pupils were forced to go further than their American teacher in the light of the latter's experience. This additional safeguard was, however, not without its price, since it brought with it the tendency for constitutional jurisdiction to become too deeply involved in dealing with political issues. In the Federal Republic of Germany especially, it has not proved possible to develop a *political question doctrine* along American lines.

It appears to be no coincidence that in a survey carried out in 1983 only two judges at the constitutional court were in favour of adopting the political question doctrine[37] and that the acceptance of its equivalent in the decision on the Kalkar nuclear facility and in the more recent cases of complaints against the dissolution of the *Bundestag* and the deployment of missiles seems to be more of an implicit and gradual process.[38] In foreign policy, this trend had always been greater. In the judgment on the Basic Treaty with the German Democratic Republic, for instance, there were signs of the development of a political-question doctrine.[39] The term 'doctrine' gives the misleading impression that there is a clearly defined discipline in America. The so-called doctrine is, however, used in a watered-down form in many decisions.[40]

Although the political question doctrine was often recommended in Germany in the hope that it would make the judges more restrained, American experience does show that the application of the doctrine is far from being a panacea. In America it could not hold the Supreme Court back from giving a decision on highly political issues either.[41] On occasions, the Supreme Court's decisions have aggravated social conflicts. The Dred–Scott decision (on former slaves returning to a state where slavery was still practised) is regarded as one of the triggers of the Civil War.[42]

The degree of activity of the Supreme Court in the USA has gone through different phases, despite the development of the political question doctrine. A number of American writers regard this as an unsolved structural problem. The courts are remote from reality and the facts of life and often have to deal with much too small a segment of that reality.[43] That explains the oscillating waves of impact on the political process: 'either too fast or too slow' – but never at quite the right pace. In Germany the fluctuations are less; the over-concise statement quoted above could hardly be applied to the judges in Karlsruhe. Social conditions are also more uniform in a smaller country; however, the constitutional demands for the standardization of living conditions have also been more firmly structured in advance by the Basic Law. A minimum of 'social democratic consensus' with an egalitarian impulse lay behind the Basic Law, one which fits the American vital consciousness in the social sphere to a much lesser extent – however much egalitarianism in the legal sphere in America was otherwise much further developed than in the continental countries with their numerous relicts of a former rigid class structure.

The influence of the Supreme Court on public policy was predominantly negative. Reforms (such as those put forward by the Warren Court) were only possible with the cooperation of the other organs of state.[44] It was scarcely possible to force the implementation of executive decisions. It was much more often the case that the Supreme Court delayed the implementation of government decisions by a matter of decades. It is true that the Legislator does have means available to obviate obstruction by the Court, such as *amending the Constitution*. Outmanoeuvring Court decisions by means of constitutional amendment is, however, likely to succeed all the more infrequently, the more difficult the amendment procedure is in itself. In America this has only happened four times in the course of history.[45]

The American model of the Supreme Court has not been so influential in its entirety, although individual of its institutions have. In Germany there was much resistance to adopting the 'dissenting vote'. It was only introduced by means of a reform in 1970. In the comparative literature, the influence of the 'proliferation of judicial opinion-writing' has been broadly welcomed, especially in Anglo-Saxon Commonwealth countries, since it has brought flexibility into constitutional law.[46]

The fact that the dissenting vote originated in Anglo-Saxon legal circles, which were less used to thinking in terms of hierarchy and career,[47] did admittedly have the effect that the adoption of this American institution in Switzerland and in Germany led to less 'heated judicial dissent' than was feared.

Notes

1   Karl Loewenstein: *Der Staatspräsident*, in: ibid: *Beiträge zur Staatsoziologie*, Tübingen, Mohr, 1961 (331-396), p. 332, note 1.

2   Kenneth C. Wheare: *Federal Government*, Oxford UP, London, 1963, 4th edn. pp. 53ff.

3   Vladimir Tumanov: *Pochemu v Sovetskom Soyuze net konstitutsionnogo suda*, Moscow, 1985 (hectographed).

4   cf Donald P. Kommers: *Judicial Review in Italy and West Germany*, JÖR, 30, 1981, pp. 1124-33; Carl J. Friedrich: Representation and Constitutional Reform in Europe. *Western Political Quarterly 1948* (124-130) p. 124.

5   Rudolf Smend: in: *Das Bundesverfassungsgericht* Karlsruhe, C.F. Müller, 1963, p. 27.

6   Ulrich Scheuner: *Die Überlieferung der deutschen Staatsgerichtsbarkeit im 19. und 20. Jahrhundert*, in: Christian Stark (ed.): *Bundesverfassungsgericht und Grundgesetz*, Tübingen, Mohr, Vol. 1, 1976 (1-62) pp. 10f; Friedrich Kühn: *Formen des verfassungsgerichtlichen Rechtsschutzes im deutschen Reichs- und Landesstaatsrecht*, Leipzig, Weicher, 1929, passim.

7   Fritz Fleiner/Z. Giacometti: *Schweizerisches Bundesstaatsrecht*, Zurich, Polygraphischer Verlag, 1965, Reprint, p. 887; Z. Giacometti: *Die Verfassungsgerichtsbarkeit des Schweizerischen Bundesgerichtes*, Zurich, Polygraphischer Verlag, 1933, pp. 27ff.

8   Alexander Hamilton et al.: *The Federalist or the New Constitution*, London, Everyman, 1948, p. 394 (Federalist Paper No. 78).

9   citing René Marcic: *Verfassung und Verfassungsgerichtsbarkeit*, Vienna, Springer, 1963, p. 204.

10   Mauro Cappelletti/Theodor Ritterspach: *Die gerichtliche Kontrolle der Verfassungsmäßigkeit der Gesetze in rechtsvergleichender Betrachtung*. JÖR, 1971, (65-109) pp. 90f.

11   cf Hans Joachim Faller: *Die Verfassungsgerichtsbarkeit in der Frankfurter Nationalversammlung*. Festschrift für Willi Geiger, Tübingen, Mohr, 1974, pp. 827-866.

12   Rudolf Hübner (ed.): *Aktenstücke und Aufzeichnungen zur Geschichte der Frankfurter Nationalversammlung aus dem Nachlass von Johann Gustav Droysen*, Stuttgart, DVA, 1924, p. 136.

13   Franz Wigard (ed.) *Stenographischer Bericht über die Verhandlungen der deutschen constituirenden Nationalversammlung zu Frankfurt am Main, Frankfurt, 1848,* Vol. 5, p. 3609, col. 1 and Vol. 8, p. 5687, col. 1.

14   Idem, Vol. 5, p. 3614, col. 1.

15   Idem, Vol. 5, p. 3616, col. 1.

16   Scheuner, op. cit. p. 30.

17   Citing Faller, op. cit., p. 831.

18   James C. Macpherson: *The Potential Implications of Constitutional Reform for the Supreme Court of Canada,* in: Stanley M. Beck/Ivan Bernier (eds.): *Canada and the New Constitution,* Montreal, The Institute for Research on Public Policy, 1983, Vol. 1 (161-223), p. 168; Ronald G. Landes: *The Canadian Polity. A comparative Introduction,* Scarborough, Prentice Hall of Canada, 1983, p. 418.

19   Keith Banting/Richard Simeon: *And No One Cheered. Federalism, Democracy and The Constitution Act,* Toronto, Methuen, 1983, p. 89.

20   Alexander Brady: *Democracy in the Dominions,* Toronto, UP 1947, 1955, p. 157.

21   Cappelletti/Ritterspach, op. cit. p. 84.

22   Rudolf Aladár Métall: *Hans Kelsen. Leben und Werk.* Vienna, Deuticke, 1969, p. 35.

23   Hans Kelsen (ed.): *Der Verfassungsgesetze der Republik Österreich. Teil 5.* Vienna, Deuticke, 1922, p. 55.

24   René Marcic: *Verfassungsgerichtsbarkeit und Reine Rechtslehre,* Vienna, Deuticke, 1966, p. 56.

25   Herbert Haller: *Hans Kelsen – Schöpfer der verfassungsgerichtlichen Gesetzesprüfung?* Arbeitshefte der Wirtschaftsuniversität Wien, Reihe Rechtswissenschaft, No. 4, 1977, p. 92; On the dogmatic tradition in the German-speaking world: Christoph Gusy: *Richterliches Prüfungsrecht. Eine verfassungsgeschichtliche Untersuchung,* Berlin, Duncker & Humblot, 1985.

26   Manfried Welan: *Der Verfassungsgerichtshof – eine Nebenregierung?* In: Heinz Fischer (ed.): *Das politische System Österreichs,* Vienna, Europaverlag, 1977, 2nd Edition (271-316) p. 283.

27   Cappelletti/Ritterspach, op. cit. p. 86, Rudolf Heinrich Grossmann: *Die staats- und rechtsideologischen Grundlagen der Verfassungsgerichtsbarkeit in den Vereinigten Staaten von Amerika und in der Schweiz,* Zurich, Schulthess, 1948, pp. 121ff.

28   Rudolf Dolzer: *Die staatstheoretische und staatsrechtliche Stellung des Bundesverfassungsgerichts,* Berlin, Duncker & Humblot, 1972, p. 39.

29   Helmut Ridder: *In Sachen Opposition.* In: Festschrift für Adolf Arndt zum 65. Geburtstag, Frankfurt, EVA, 1969, (323-348) p. 333.

30   Parlamentarischer Rat: *Stenographischer Bericht über die Plenarsitzungen,* Bonn 1948/49, p. 25, col. 2.

31   Hans Kelsen: *Wer soll der Hüter der Verfassung sein?* Berlin, Rothschild, 1931, p. 36.

32   Dolzer, op. cit., p. 37.

33   Hans Kelsen: *Wesen und Entwicklung der Staatsgerichtsbarkeit,* VVDStRL, H. 5 Berlin, De Gruyter, 1929, p. 85, 87.

34   Walter Strauss: *Der oberste Bundesgerichtshof,* Heidelberg, Lambert Schneider, 1949, p. 28.

35   Heinz Laufer: *Verfassungsgerichtsbarkeit und politischer Prozess,* Tübingen, Mohr, 1968, pp. 38ff.

36   Cappelletti/Ritterspach, op. cit., p. 101.

37   Christine Landfried: *Bundesverfassungsgerichtsbarkeit und Gesetzgeber.*

Wirkungen der Verfassungsrechtsprechung auf die parlamentarische Willensbildung und die soziale Realität, Baden-Baden, Nomos, 1984, p. 153.

38   cf Rudolf Dolzer: *Verfassungskonkretisierung durch das Bundesverfassungsgericht und durch politische Verfassungsorgane*, Heidelberg, H.v.Decker/C.F. Müller, 1982, pp. 29ff.

39   Christian Tomuschat: *Auswärtige Gewalt und verfassungsrichterliche Kontrolle*, DöV, 1973, p. 801.

40   Fritz Wilhelm Scharpf: *Grenzen der richterlichen Verantwortung*, Karlsruhe, C.F. Müller, 1965, p. 404f.

41   Samuel Krislow: *The Supreme Court in the Political Process*, New York/London, MacMillan-Collier, 1965, p. 96.

42   Stephen L. Wasby: *The Impact of the United States Supreme Court: Some Perspectives*, H. Homewood/Ill. Dorsey Press, 1970, p. 6f.

43   Alexander H. Bickel: *The Supreme Court and the Idea of Progress*, New Haven, Yale UP, 2nd Edn. 1979, p. 175.

44   Archibald Cox: *The Role of the Supreme Court in American Government*, Oxford, Clarendon, 1976, pp. 76f.

45   John Hart Ely: *Democracy and Distrust. A Theory of Judicial Review*, Cambridge/Mass., Harvard UP, 1982, 2nd edn., p.46.

46   Edward McWhinney: *Federal Constitutional Courts and Their Judges, as Instruments of a Democratic Polity*, in: Karl Dietrich Bracher et al. (eds.): *Die moderne Demokratie und ihr Recht*. Festschrift für Gerhard Leibholz zum 65. Geburtstag, Tübingen, Mohr, 1966, Vol. 2 (513-530), p. 517.

47   Hans Georg Rupp: *Zur Frage der Dissenting Opinion*, idem Vol. 2 (531-549). p. 532.

5 Institutions of Representation and Participation

There is no country where the major American institutions have been taken over *in toto*. But with America's increasing leadership role the American model has become the object of more and more serious study. America became influential as the result of the adoption of many partial aspects of its institutions of representation and participation and some critics even in America itself appear to regard this influence as excessive:

> With the United States of America such a 'hegemonic' power in some academic disciplines this has meant in recent times that the particular – not to say peculiar – configuration of its regime structures has often been taken for 'the' model of conformity to the citizenship principle (a strange choice in my view), given that country's decidedly inferior performance on a number of key indicators such as high voting abstention, restrictive registration practices, weak unionization, low competition for many legislative seats, barriers to the formation of new parties, and so forth.[1]

It was particularly the less formalized areas of political participation which Schmitter judged negatively but it transpires that the exemplary role in this area is rather modest, being limited to certain aspects of parliamentary life and election primaries. Most aspects of elections, parties and lobbies have tended to remain alien to other countries, right through to the American 'soap-powder' election, even if certain techniques of campaign management have been imitated. Within the *parliamentary sphere* many of the practices belong to the admired and frequently copied institutions, such as the system of hard-working committees, the conference committees as a form of arbitration, the sub-committees or the hearings.

Italy was inspired by the 'joint committees'[2] and both Italy and Germany introduced hearings with a quite deliberate reference to America. In the case of the Mediation Committee (*Vermittlungsausschuss*), the invention of which was ascribed to Adenauer, those members of the Committee of Five whom it was still possible to ask about its origin admit the overriding influence of the American model: To quote Menzel: 'Foreign models were decisive', or Carlo Schmid: 'To begin with, I did not think of foreign models. However, while attempting to find a possible concrete solution for conflicts between the two organs, the *Bundesrat* and the *Bundestag*, I came across the American model.'[3]

Some of the copies managed to become fully adapted in Europe; in non-European democracies they remained foreign bodies. A case in point would be the committee system which made its way into the rules of procedure of the Japanese Parliament, borrowing heavily on the American Legislative Reorganization Act of 1946. The effects came nowhere near to those of the American model. A comparative study on the use of committees came to the conclusion:

> Thus, the strongest committee system in our study (the American) became the weakest (the Japanese) in the course of transplantation. This example adds to existing evidence that efforts by colonial or occupying powers to impose their governmental arrangements in alien settings carry no guarantee of success.[4]

Taken as a whole, the American *party system* has aroused neither admiration nor desires to copy it in the rest of the world. Despite the frequent comparison between the two-party systems in the USA and Great Britain, the British model remained the more influential.

Even in America, the resigned recognition that it was not possible to carry through a radical reform of the presidential system led to change via reforms in the party system. A large part of reform proposals is characterized by distrust of institutional changes in the relationship between the powers. It seeks to integrate the two most important powers, not by changing the Constitution nor by reforming Parliament but by binding the two together through the parties and aiming to expand 'responsible party government'.

Ever since Woodrow Wilson there had been a call for 'party government' in America, and the British party system was often put forward as an example to follow. Wilson and A. Lawrence Lowell were the first major adversaries in the party discussion. Lowell had a certain sympathy for the British system but, since he regarded it as impossible to transplant that system to America, he was also suspicious of Wilson's party doctrine as being excessively 'parliamentarian'. One of the arguments he used against Wilson has been taken up repeatedly right up until the present day: the British party system, it is claimed, includes such a strong inclination towards majoritization that it would be barely compatible with the American Constitution and the deep concern to protect minority interests.[5]

In the controversial report of the 'American Political Science Association' (an appalling example of expert policy masquerading under the authority of a full-scale scientific association) the people were criticized in a paternalistic manner. English myths of a rationally activistic form of politics without the 'swamp of unideological interest politics' were reproduced in this report without the slightest inhibition.

The report simply failed to comprehend that the American party system reflected the fear of majority tyranny, which was also the basis of the constitutional institutions, and that such aversions could not be dispelled simply by means of a few institutional changes, however well-intentioned.[6]

As the older institutionalistic school was gradually replaced this particular debate was also abandoned. It had been a hapless attempt to find a compromise in the old discussion of 'presidential versus parliamentary form of government', in the full knowledge that a parliamentarization of the American system stood no chance at all (cf. Chapter 2).

With the behaviouralist wave, the whole line of argument appeared to swing round in favour of the American model. The demise of the American parties now looked like a sign of maturity. When it came to parties and elections it was less the institutions of the 'American model' that were influential and more the interpretative patterns established by American field research. Europe began to ask whether it would also become affected by the waning party identification.

The more a European system moved away from the American two-party model, for which the hypothesis of *party identification* had been developed, the greater grew the danger of tautological results. In many European democracies socio-structural determinants of political behaviour brought about a greater degree of agreement between party identification and voting habits. Both factors were, however, more dependent on a third parameter than was the case in America.

It seemed easiest of all to apply the concept of party identification to Great Britain. It is a concept used by Butler and Stokes; however, they were more cautious and coined the term 'partisan self-images' in order not to read too much into party identification. Even in Britain, these self-images showed greater agreement with electoral preferences than in the USA.[7]

Switching parties in Europe was more often preceded by a change in lasting loyalty towards the party than in America. But here again, a number of forecasts were not fulfilled. Butler and Stokes had regarded it as possible that identification with the two big parties in Great Britain could increase still further, since identification with the Liberals was on the wane. The opposite actually happened and the number of floating voters increased.[8] Contrary to what happened in most other countries, the two big parties' share of the poll in Great Britain fell from 77.4 per cent (in 1950) to 53.7 per cent (in October 1974). The turnout also fell: the assumption that party identification is a learning process which only evolves in stages as one political generation follows the other, was opened to challenge by rapid social developments in England.[9] 'Partisan dealignment' also took hold of the British electorate. However, it began to occur later than in the USA. Although the two major parties' share of the poll fell continuously, party identification held up throughout the sixties and was not seriously breached until 1974. In the case of the Conservatives, these losses appeared to be caused by individual events (EC membership), whereas in the case of Labour, longer-term trends were detected, such as many electors' dissatisfaction with the role of the trades unions in the party and in society. As far as the Labour Party is concerned, the social composition of its voters changed more quickly than did that of the Conservatives. In the seventies, it was still true that the majority came from a working-class background, but the number of middle-class voters in the party increased. The idea that it was the younger generation in particular which was one of the main causes for falling party loyalty, on account of its greater reluctance to identify with a single political party (a repeated finding in older studies), is something which cannot be said in the case of Great Britain.[10]

The concept of party loyalty has also been adopted in the Federal Republic of Germany. Views on its value have fluctuated with time. To begin with, it appeared it could be used without restriction. In Germany, even more citizens identified with the parties (76.5 per cent) than in America (72.5 per cent).[11] In the early seventies there was increasing controversy over the value of party identification and it was not until the end of the seventies that interest in the concept as an analytical tool began to grow again but in a more discriminating form. On many occasions the talk was more of 'affective party orientation' rather than party identification.[12] Apart from affective components, cognitive factors also played a part, especially in terms of 'issue competence', that is the ability of parties and politicians to solve major problems.

Changing values, new social movements and the collapse of the parties' organizational power once the wave of participation in the early seventies had declined appeared to make the American pattern of interpretation ever more applicable. However, it cannot be claimed that this trend was deliberately promoted, even in the conservative middle-class parties. On the contrary, it was above all the Christian Democratic parties in Europe, such as the DC and the CDU, which at that time especially showed that they were capable of widening their organizations to become firmly institutionalized mass parties.

There were also other areas of political party life where the European development took a different course to that in America. Whereas many American provisions acted as sources of inspiration in the lobby regulation, in the area of *party finances* Europe has tended rather to move further away from America. This is one of the few areas where there was actually still such a thing as an Anglo-Saxon tradition, and this had led to the separate development of two quite different models:

1   The *Anglo-Saxon* model tries to sustain competition in the political market place by setting ceilings on party expenditure.

2   The *continental European* model tries to satisfy the parties' hunger for funding by giving public electoral subsidies, but this does not completely eliminate financial scandals.

It is only in the area of campaign expenditure for presidential elections that there has so far been some closing of the gap between the two models.[13] The fact is, however, that public subsidization of parties does only partially eliminate financial scandals and corruption, and that is precisely why the American experiences with 'financial disclosure' and the limitation of campaign expenditure are gradually supplementing the continental policy of subsidization.

When it comes to *interest groups*, the move away from the American interpretative model was slower than in the area of party research. American theories of pluralism taken from the Bentley and Truman school dominated the postwar scene, especially in Germany. Neopluralists such as Ernst Fraenkel, returning from a period of emigration, had replaced the class conflict models of the Weimar period with pluralist models of American origin.[14] It became increasingly obvious, however, that these models were even wider off the mark as regards the facts of life in Europe than in America. Americans carrying out research into Europe found they could do very little with Bentleyism in 'Non-American field situations'. The discovery of *parentela* and *clientela* structures in Italy led to the recognition that public administrations were not merely arenas and that bureaucrats were less arbitrators and more participants in the conflict of interests.[15] It is thus no wonder that, given the stronger *étatiste* tradition in continental Europe, pluralist theories were forced to yield ground virtually without a fight in favour of the neo-corporatist type of explanation, which even today still provides a powerful explanation for the cooperation between the state and interest groups in many European countries, but hardly so in the case of America.[16]

These divergences in the area of societal organizations do not, however, mean that America did not, all the same, develop as a model which was copied in certain areas. The less formal types of association, the *citizens' action groups* and *public interest groups*, not representing their own interests but those of less articulate social groups, also acted as models for Europe. Ralph Nader–style advocacy politics or public interest groups, such as Common Cause, have not really been able to develop functional equivalents to the American example in systems which are less open for the articulation of interests. An absolutely negative image from the European point of view is represented by the American model of *industrial relations*. It is only the employers who see America (and Japan) as an example worth following. The business unions, in their fragmentation and the different nature of their relationships with the political parties, have not met with any large measure of understanding elsewhere in the world, let alone a desire to copy them.[17] The weakness of the trades unions and their low level of prestige among the population at large, where they are not liked and are, at best, accepted as an essential element of democratic pluralism, cannot act as an example abroad.[18]

American literature on industrial relations was very often much more strongly on the defensive than that on party research. At best, it was established that: 'American unionism has been maturing, and the features of institutional middle age should be increasingly evident in the years ahead.'[19]

America fought successfully for political and economic rights earlier than many European countries. The tendency for an initially repressive government policy to make a complete turnabout into an intensive policy of cooperation as soon as government bodies needed the trades unions, which led to liberal corporatism, is thus absent in America. The lack of feudal traditions and the openness of the political system were proffered as an explanation for the American variety of industrial relations.[20] The 'archaic' features of the American system of industrial relations are thus sometimes even described as the 'more mature' and the collectivism, the high degree of organization and the politicization of the labour movement in Europe are explained rather in terms of 'lingering aspects of precapitalist culture', which would not exactly encourage the conclusion that these aspects of working life could become the example for future post-industrial societies.[21]

Seen in this light, it is possible to explain the habit among neoconservatives of declaring the 'rearguard' of the labour movement to be the 'vanguard' of the world of tomorrow. If this view were to win the day, then the American system of industrial relations could develop as an influential model for the future – beyond the limited circle of organized employers. Given the European traditions of the social state, however, this seems rather unlikely.

American democracy faced two different kinds of difficulty in adjusting its archaic system of institutions. These had to stand up to the erupting social conflicts after the New Deal and they had to be adapted to America's role as a world power. It is no wonder that this did not happen without friction. Domestic criticism of the institutions of American democracy was too severe for these to be able to develop any effective generalized exemplary function in the conflicts of the sixties and seventies.

The American model did, however, benefit from a methodological change in paradigm and the old institutionalism was replaced by the *behaviouralist revolt*. It was now possible to combine the methodologically useful with the ideologically desirable. Research into the political behaviour of Americans using survey techniques produced a significantly more favourable picture of American democracy than the descriptive and normative comparison of institutions had done. Political science throughout the world became a 'penetrated system', which readily adopted the American pattern of interpretation and was sometimes overhasty in regarding America's leading role in political science as synonymous with a leading role in political democracy.

This explains why it was neither the electoral system nor the parties that took on model character for Europe but those factors which filled the two of them with life and were rooted in the *political culture* of the country. But these in particular were hard to transpose and they could, at best, be learnt over the longer term. The accusation that the ideal political culture, a participatory but not excessively activistic one, had already been defined in accordance with American findings is as old as research into political culture itself. Even if that were true for the definition of 'civic culture', then the comparative investigations following Almond and Verba's pioneering study have not yet come up with conflicting results.[22]

In the area of *research into participation* it was not only the terminology and methodology of empirical social research that had model character, the USA, despite the inadequacies of its institutions, also came to be regarded as the model pupil of democracy in many transnational comparisons. The use of survey methods confirmed the old stereotypes of national character studies: 'Thus, while Americans may have had a gospel of wealth, they have never had – and, in the nature of things, cannot have – a gospel of power.'[23]

Since there was no need for a state to counteract feudalistic fragmentation, America had little experience of centralizing government

Table 5.1: The Feeling of National Pride

	B	DK	D	F	IRL	I	L	NL	UK	GR	USA 1981	Japan 1981	Spain 1981
April 1983													
Very proud	24	39	17	36	52	40	51	34	57	76	80	30	49
Quite proud	44	39	39	39	34	44	37	44	35	16	15	32	34
Not very proud	17	10	24	14	7	10	4	12	5	4	2	28	8
Not at all proud	4	2	9	5	3	4	2	4	2	2	1	3	4
Don't know	11	10	11	6	4	2	6	6	1	2	2	7	5
Total	100	100	100	100	100	100	100	100	100	100	100	100	100

Sources: 1983: Eurobarometre, No. 19, 1983, p. 54; 1981: International Study on Values 1981/82, Allensbach.

Table 5.2: Electoral participation in parliamentary (PA) and presidential (PR) elections (1945-1982)

Country	Number of elections	Mean	Rank order	Turnout (in %) Highest	Turnout (in %) Lowest	Coefficient of last election variation[a]
Countries where voting is compulsory[b]						
Austria (PR)[c]	7	95.2	1	1957:97.2	1980:91.6	1980:91.6	1.99
Belgium (PA)	13	92.1	5	1977:95.1	1981:87.7	1981:87.7	2.33
Greece (PA)[d]	12	78.6	18	1963:83.0	1958:72.0	1981:78.7	4.70
Italy (PA)	9	92.4	4	1958:93.8	1946:89.1	1979:90.4	1.75
Luxembourg (PA)[e]	9	90.7	6	1959:92.3	1968:88.5	1979:88.9	1.58
The Netherlands until 1970 (PA)	7	94.7	2	1959:95.6	1946:93.1	1967:94.9	0.99
Countries where voting is not compulsory[f]						
Austria (PA)	11	94.0	3	1949:96.8	1970:91.8	1979:92.3	1.74
Canada (PA)	13	75.4	22	1958:80.5	1953:67.8	1980:69.3	5.31
Denmark (PA)	16	85.6	13	1969:89.3	1953:80.6	1981:82.6	3.39
Finland (PR)	6	73.3	24	1982:86.6	1950:63.8	1982:86.6	12.58
Finland (PA)	11	78.7	17	1962:85.1	1975:73.8	1979:75.3	5.41
France (PR)[g]	4	81.4	14	1974:87.8	1969:69.1	1981:84.0	10.26
France (PA)[h]	12	78.7	17	1956/78:82.7	1962:68.8	1981:71.4	5.54
FRG (PA)	9	87.1	10	1972:91.1	1949:78.5	1980:88.6	4.21
Iceland (PR)	3	88.2	9	1968:92.2	1952:82.0	1980:90.5	6.19
Iceland (PA)	12	90.1	7	1956:92.1	1946/53:87.4	1979:89.3	1.68
Ireland (PA)[i]	12	74.2	23	1969:76.9	1961:69.9	II/1982:72.8	3.07
Israel (PR)	10	81.1	15	1949:86.9	1951:75.1	1981:78.5	4.36
Japan (PA)	15	72.8	25	1958:77.0	1947/79:68.0	1980:74.5	3.98
The Netherlands (PA)	12	90.0	8	1959:95.6	1971:78.5	1982:80.6	7.08

Norway (PA)	10	81.1	1965:85.4	1945:76.4	3.49	1981:83.2
Portugal (PR)	2	79.9	1980:84.2	1976:75.5	7.70	1980:84.2
Portugal (PA)j	4	86.7	1975:91.7	1976:83.3	4.36	1980:84.3
Spain (PA)	3	75.5	1982:79.5	1979:68.0	8.64	1982:79.5
Sweden (PA)	12	85.9	1976:91.8	1958:77.4	6.06	1982:91.4
Switzerland (PA)	9	62.7	1947:71.7	1979:48.1	13.34	1979:48.1
Turkey (PA)	9	77.1	1950:89.3	1969:64.3	11.66	1977:72.4
United Kingdom (PA)	11	77.0	1950:83.9	1970:72.0	5.00	1979:75.9
The USA (PR)k	9	58.0	1960:62.8	1948:51.1	7.32	1980:53.9
The USA (PA)	19	46.8	1960:58.5	1978:35.1	16.10	1982:ca.41

a   Multiplied by 100.
b   Except for the case of Italy sanctions against non-voters are possible. In Italy 'did not vote' is stamped on the identification papers of abstainers. In addition voting is made more attractive by generous concessions on train fares available to those who have to return to their home constituency to vote.
c   First ballot.
d   There is a duty to vote for citizens who are between 21 and 70 years of age and who are not further away than 200 km from their constituency on election day. Not included here are the elections of 1946 (turnout 59.7 per cent), which took place in a situation of civil war; and of 1950 (no data available).
e   No data for 1945.
f   Voting is compulsory, however, in some parts of Switzerland (Cantons: Aargau, Schaffhausen, St Gallen, Thurgau) and Austria (States: Tirol, Vorarlberg, Steiermark).
g   Second ballot.
h   First ballot.
i   Presidential elections are only held if the parties in parliament cannot agree on a candidate for the presidency. Competitive elections with turnout rates of about 60 per cent took place between 1945 and 1973.
j   The election for the constitutional assembly of 1975 is included.
k   Valid votes only, as a percentage of the voting age population.

Source: R. Sturm: 'Wahlbeteiligung', in: M.G. Schmidt (ed.), Westliche Industriegesellschaften, Munich, Piper, 1983 (475-481), p. 478 f.

power. The belief in the system, for all the scepticism shown towards those in power at the time and towards several of the institutions, was praised as a characteristic of America's political culture. The fact that America, with 80 per cent of its population very proud another 15 per cent proud of the American nation (see Table 5.1) has never fallen into hypertrophic nationalism, and intoxication with power is ascribed to the aloof attitude vis-à-vis the government of the day, the critical attitude towards the institutions and the participant political culture. Negative results which can be put down to this (for instance, electoral turnout, where America comes out at the bottom of the league table compared with other democracies – see Table 5.2) used to be played down as an artificial product of institutional circumstances (such as the mandatory registration procedure).[24]

In the meantime that is hardly credible any more, given falling turn-out figures, and the social reasons for not voting must be given stronger weighting. America was always able to console itself over the low turn-out figures by the fact that measured in terms of other indicators of conventional behaviour (canvassing, party donations, readers' letters) it ranked above all the other Western democracies. But there are still problems, given that in the light of the weakness of party organization these compensatory activities cannot necessarily be compared with the much more bureaucratic nature of the involvement of Europeans in their countries' political parties.

In later analyses, it was also found that the USA had the lowest figures for non-political findings and that America had the most positive findings for many other indicators. The fact that the American pattern of participation, however, moved furthest away from a system of clearly defined conflict groups was no longer ascribed as the product of unique historical circumstances or of political culture. It was assumed that the USA once resembled the fragmentation of the Netherlands or Austria and that the two consociational democracies would also develop towards an ever-increasing openness in their system.[25]

Whereas the groups who advocated new forms of political behaviour could see this as a hope which could lead to more equality of participation, Verba and his colleagues are sceptical about this trend which started in America: 'The result may, however, be less rather than more political equality.'[26] For the time being, this is, however, only an assumption, which cannot be confirmed by a comparison of surveys carried out to date.[27]

The controversy does, however, show that in participation research the appraisal of American developments also oscillates between two poles. On some occasions America is viewed as an atypical case, on others it is seen as a pioneer of all post-industrial societies, being merely the first country to go through the inevitable process of social change.

Left-wing criticism of research into political culture and participation has often put forward the argument that its fundamental terminology was based on typical American and rather quietistic values. Research into unconventional behaviour has overcome this shortcoming. America was still the leading participant culture with the lowest numbers of inactive citizens (cf. Tables 5.3 and 5.4). In an international study, America emerged as the leader of the new 'political versatility':

> Thus, our statement that America is a truly participant culture can be further differentiated by observing that a marriage of conventional and unconventional participation has taken place to an extent that precludes any doubts with regard to the within-system status of direct action techniques.[28]

At all events, America no longer came out top for all the indicators. For unconventional patterns of behaviour and sensitivity to government sanctions against protest behaviour, the Netherlands not only approached America but even surpassed the American values.

Although the focus was a different one, this finding tallied with Ingelhart's discovery that, when it came to the number of post-materialists, the USA lagged behind Belgium and the Netherlands,[29] since there are certain affinities between postmaterialism and unconventional behaviour. That does not mean that all unconventional be-

Table 5.3: Empirical balance between modes of political involvement

Political Style	The Netherlands	Britain	United States	Germany	Austria
Political Apathy	13%	23%	8%	16%	25%
Political Detachment	5	7	5	11	10
Expressive Political Action	29	32	22	19	18
Instrumental Political Action	53	38	65	54	47
Total	100	100	100	100	100
(N=)	(1136)	(1378)	(1605)	(2203)	(1264)

Source: Samuel H. Barnes, Max Kaase et al.: *Political Action*. Beverly Hills, Sage, 1979, p. 528.

Table 5.4: Political Action Repertory typology restructured: the modes of political action

		The Netherlands	Britain	United States	Germany	Austria
A.	Modes of Political Action					
	None (Inactives)	18=%	30	12	27	35
	Only Conventional (Reformists)	11	15	18	13	19
	Mixed Mode (Reformists and Activists)	39	33	50	33	27
	Only Unconventional (Protesters)	32	22	20	27	19
	(N=)	(1144)	(1389)	(1613)	(2207)	(1265)
B.	Lack of Involvement in:*					
	Unconventional Politics	9=%	23	9	18	21
	Conventional Politics	29	28	16	23	34

* Percentage of scalable respondents with 'O' value on the respective scale.
Source: Samuel H. Barnes, Max Kaase et al.: *Political Action*. Beverly Hills, Sage, 1979, p.528.

haviour results from postmaterial sets of values, as is shown by anomic forms of participation in less developed countries.

The most important change to have been observed in American political culture since the civic culture study was a *collapse of confidence in politics and the political institutions*.[30] There are insufficient comparative studies which ask the same questions and use the same scale. The pride in American political institutions, which was once measured at 85 per cent, compared with 46 per cent in Great Britain, 7 per cent in Germany and 3 per cent in Italy (cf. Table 5.5), has obviously declined. Any comparison carried out in the eighties into the attitude towards individual institutions in the USA and in the Federal Republic of Germany will show that the universities and the media score markedly higher in America. Germany is still not in a position to give the complete lie to the verdict of having more of a 'legalistic' and less of a 'participant' disposition, if consideration is given to the high margin by which the greatest degree of confidence is expressed in the Federal Constitutional Court.

It is, however, not possible to draw all that many conclusions, given the different composition of the institutions about which questions were put and the differences in the scales used.

The most important difference would, however, appear to be that America reacts more quickly and more thoroughly to errors in the institutions than do most European countries. The gap between missionary awareness and ideals, on the one hand, and political reality, on the other, is thus subject to periodic changes which have led astray many forecasts of the future of the American model.

Table 5.5: Aspects of nation in which respondents report pride, by nation (in per cent)

Per cent who say they are proud of	U.S.	U.K.	Germany	Italy	Mexico
Governmental, political institutions	85	46	7	3	30
Social legislation	13	18	6	1	2
Position in international affairs	5	11	5	2	3
Economic system	23	10	33	3	24
Characteristics of people	7	18	36	11	15
Spiritual virtues and religion	3	1	3	6	8
Contributions to the arts	1	6	11	16	9
Contributions to science	3	7	12	3	1
Physical attributes of country	5	10	17	25	22
Nothing or don't know	4	10	15	27	16
Other	9	11	3	21	14
Total % of responses*	158	148	148	118	144
Total % of respondents	100	100	100	100	100
Total number of cases	970	963	955	995	1,007

* Percentages exceed one hundred because of multiple responses.

Source: Gabriel A. Almond/Sidney Verba: *The Civic Culture*. Princeton UP, 1963, p. 102.

Table 5.6: Popular confidence in major institutions of society

	USA	GB	Ireland	France	Germany	Italy	Average
	%	%	%	%	%	%	%
Government							
Police	76	86	86	64	71	68	75
Armed forces	81	81	75	53	54	58	67
Legal system	51	66	57	66	67	43	58
Education system	65	60	67	55	43	56	58
Parliament	53	40	51	48	53	31	46
Civil service	55	48	54	50	35	28	45
Average	64	64	65	56	54	47	58
Non-governmental institutions							
Church	74	38	78	43	38	60	55
Major companies	50	48	49	42	34	38	43
Press	49	29	44	31	33	46	39
Trade unions	33	26	36	36	36	28	32
Average	33	35	52	38	35	43	39

Source: R. Rose: *Understanding Big Government*, London, Sage, 1984, p. 180.

Notes

1   Philippe C. Schmitter: *The Consolidation of Political Democracy in Southern Europe*, Florence, EUI, 1985, p. 11.
2   Carlo Chimenti: *Gli organi bicamerali nel parlamento italiano*, Milan, Comunità, 1979, pp. 342ff.
3   Letters cited in: Harri Reinert: *Vermittlungsausschuss und Conference Committees*, Heidelberg, Winter, 1966, p. 111.
4   John D. Lees/Malcolm Shaw (eds.): *Committees in Legislatures. A Comparative Analysis*, Durham, Duke UP, 1979, p. 390.
5   A. Lawrence Lowell: *Essays on Government*, Boston, 1889, pp. 63ff.
6   American Political Science Association: *Toward a More Responsible Two-Party System*, New York, Rinehart, 1950. Critique: E.M. Kirkpatrick: *Toward a More Responsible Party System. Political Science, Policy Science, or Pseudo-Science*, in: J. Fishel (ed.): *Parties and Elections in Anti-Party Age*, Bloomington, Indiana UP, 1978, p. 33-54; Austin Ranney: Toward a More Responsible Two-Party System. A Commentary, *APSR*, 1951, pp. 488-499.
7   David Butler/D. Stokes: *Political Change in Britain*, New York, St. Martins, 1976, p. 24.

8   Samuel E. Finer: *The Changing British Party System 1945-1979*, Washington, AEI, 1980, pp. 67f.

9   Ivor Crewe: *Party Identification Theory and Political Change in Britain*, in: Ian Budge et al (eds): *Party Identification and Beyond*, London, Wiley, 1976 (33-61) p. 59.

10 Ivor Crewe et al: Partisan Dealignment in Britain 1964-1974. *British Journal of Political Science*, 1977 (129-190) pp. 182ff.

11 W. Zolnhöfer: *Parteiidentifizierung in der Bundesrepublik und in den Vereinigten Staaten.* in: Erwin Scheuch, Rudolf Wildenmann (eds): *Zur Soziologie der Wahl*, KZFSS, Sonderheft 9, 1965 (126-168), p. 133.

12 Hans-Dieter Klingemann, Charles Taylor: *Affektive Parteiorientierung, Kanzlerkandidaten und Issues*, in: Max Kaase (ed.). *Wahlsoziologie heute*, PVS, 1977, No. 2/3, (301-347), p. 307.

13 cf Klaus von Beyme: *Political Parties in Western Democracies*, New York, St. Martins, 1985, pp. 202ff.

14 Hans Kremendahl: *Pluralismustheorie in Deutschland*, Cologne, Heggen, 1977, pp. 220ff; Winfried Steffani: *Pluralistische Demokratie*, Opladen, Leske, 1980, pp. 36ff.

15 Joseph LaPalombara: The Utility and Limitations of Interest Group Theory in Non-American Field Situations, *Journal of Politics*, 1960, pp. 29-49.

16 cf Klaus von Beyme: Neo-corporatism. A New Nut in an Old Shell, *IPSR*, 1983, pp. 173-196.

17 cf Klaus von Beyme: *Challenge to Power. Trade Unions and Industrial Relations in Capitalist Countries*, Beverly Hills, Sage, 1980, pp. 234ff.

18 Seymour Martin Lipset/William Schneider: *The Confidence Gap. Business. Labor and Government in the Public Mind*, New York, Free Press, 1983, p. 380.

19 Richard A. Lester: *As Unions Mature. An Analysis of American Unionism*, Princeton UP, 1958, p. 155.

20 Seymour M. Lipset: Radicalism or Reformism: The Sources of Working Class Politics. *APSR*, 1983, pp. 1-18, Alain Touraine et al.: *Le mouvement ouvrier*, Paris, Fayards, vol. 2. Mouvements, 1984, p. 44.

21 J. David Edelstein/Malcolm Warner: *Comparative Union Democracy*, London, Allen & Unwin, 1975, p. 8.

22 Alan I. Abramowitz: *The United States: Political Culture under Stress*, Gabriel A. Almond/Sidney Verba (eds): *The Civic Culture Revisited*, Boston, Little Brown, 1980 (177-211), p. 188.

23 Samuel P. Huntington: *American Politics: The Promise of Disharmony*, Cambridge/Mass. Belknap, 1981, p. 34.

24 Giuseppe Di Palma: *Apathy and Participation. Mass Politics in Western Society*, New York, Free Press, 1970, p. 35.

25 Sidney Verba et al.: *Participation and Political Equality*, Cambridge UP, 1978, p. 308.

26 Verba, op. cit. p. 309.

27 Klaus R. Allerbeck: *Politische Ungleichheit. Ein Acht-Nationen-Vergleich*, Opladen, Westdeutscher Verlag, 1980, p. 82.

28 Samuel H. Barnes/Max Kaase et al.: *Political Action. Mass Participation in Five Western Democracies*, Beverly Hills, Sage, 1979, p. 170.

29 Ronald Inglehart: *The Silent Revolution*, Princeton UP, 1977, p. 38.

30 Abramowitz, op. cit. p. 189.

6 The world-power role, a sense of mission and the future of the American model of democracy

> It is time for America to start learning again, to forget its dreams of inno-
> cence and superiority, and to become modest enough to accept that there
> are lessons to be learned from the rest of the world and from the facts.
> But, in order to be able to do this, a nation must first of all be ready to
> work harder at understanding its own behavioural patterns. (Michael
> Crozier: *The Trouble with America*, Berkeley, 1984, page 75).

The impact of the American revolution was only limited. In its time it
remained a peripheral event, whereas the French revolution shaped the
ideologies of the whole world. Even conservatives reached the (probably erroneous) conclusion relatively early on that there had not been a
real revolution in America. One reason for the public authorities in
Europe to take such a charitable view of the American upheaval was
that this model had not engendered any threat to the traditional order
of things in European countries. The expansion of the American model
remained limited to the Western hemisphere. Generally speaking, the
official American doctrine after Monroe was seen in Europe as a defensive one, restricted to its own hemisphere and with no sense of world
mission.

At an early stage, however, the Europeans began to wonder at a contradiction: on the one hand, the Americans regarded their institutions
as the best there were and ordained by God; yet, for that very same
reason, they remained sceptical about attempts to transpose them. Any
transfer of the American model could only have diluted this uniqueness. Latin America demonstrated that the adoption of the American

institutions did not lead to the further development of the American model but, on more occasions than one, merely evolved into a caricature of it.[1]

During the nineteenth century, few people went so far as to assume that the Americans had a sense of mission regarding their constitution. One of them was von Holst, who wrote the following passage in his monumental book about American democracy:

> It is possible to go right back to this early time and to see the first beginnings of the canonization of the Constitution. They began by seeing it as the best possible Constitution for the United States and gradually the view gained ground that it was generally valid as a model constitution.[2]

For many sceptical Europeans, the Americans' enthusiasm for their own institutions had something disarmingly naive about it: 'The Declaration of Independence and the Constitution laid down the basic principles of democracy with such clarity and single-mindedness that we came very close to viewing them as an American invention,' was the confession of one American writer. 'These sanctified documents bestow fundamental principles on us, which, thanks to their divine inspiration, are on a par with Creation, and it is, thus, neither possible to question their why and wherefore nor for them ever to become outdated. That is why we need concern ourselves no further with fundamental principles, they have been handed down to us – once and for all.'[3]

The product of this constitutional creationism has been called 'Americanism'. It is characterized by the contradiction of the awareness of a special role associated with a claim to universal applicability. Contrary to the rest of the world, political theory basically developed as 'didactics of Americanism'. Even when empirical political science came into being, it was at first characterized by a detestation of theory reminiscent of Burke. It was the study of the 'American way of life' with modest sprinklings of self-criticism. It did not contain a far-reaching political theory but rather the methodology and techniques for the dissemination of a predefined American liberalism[4]. Despite all this, the self-satisfaction did not really turn into missionary activity for the dissemination of the American model.

A necessary precondition for the development of a sense of a missionary role is the existence of a clear-cut ideology. Since, however, there were no secular conflicts between capitalism and feudalism or, later, between capitalism and socialism as in Europe, there was less of a need for a political ideology. Political theory in America was more or less a variation on the theme of 'democracy'. The basic values of the democratic credo constitute the vehicles and techniques for settling conflicts, not sets of substantive metaphysical beliefs. Consensus is a matter of procedure and not one of deeper substance. Parsons coined the phrase 'instrumental activism' for this.[5]

A central aspect of the formation of ideologies in Europe was either the criticism or the defence of ecclesiastical doctrines. In America, religion had never been a means of enforcing the authority of an absolute ruler and it was, moreover, fragmented in hundreds of different sects. Here, there was no need to draw a clear demarcation line between religious and political thought. The puritanism of the American denominations tended to blur these dividing lines.[6] Given its theoretical vagueness and religious ramifications, the democratic message resulting from America's missionary awareness was too patchy for it to win over any large number of new converts. The American credo had virtually nothing to do with the existentialism of most European ideologies, which regarded it as a collection of commonplaces.

The more American theoreticians were convinced of the quality of American institutions, the less they regarded them as capable of transplantation. As early as at the time of the Mexican War, Calhoun warned against excessive missionary zeal in contacts with more traditional societies: 'Take care that you do more to spread the cause of freedom in this country and in the world as a whole by the example we set than could be done by a thousand victories.'[7]

There were a number of falls from grace into imperialism in the course of American history, especially in the Philippines, but Theodore Roosevelt was honest enough after a few years of military engagement of American troops there to recognize that annexation was a mistake. The war with Spain and the seizure of the last of its colonies in the Western hemisphere has often been interpreted as a break with America's anti-imperialist tradition, but even the most charitable interpretation cannot avoid regarding American policy in the Caribbean since then as a compromise between rejection of European imperialism and the declaration of its own law in America's backyard[8], with the Monroe doctrine stretched even beyond the expansionist aspects it admittedly contained already. American observers of Russian imperialism have occasionally criticized the Soviet Union's self-justification, which displays a clear conscience over keeping former colonial conquests. For the Soviets, imperialism seems to be linked to the idea that 'you get there by sea' (Charles Bohlen). A similar claim could also be made regarding the USA. Its anti-imperialism was always at its strongest when the territory concerned was far away from the heartland and it appeared impossible to integrate it within the Union. In the long run, overseas imperialism was only accepted in waters near to America's borders.

After the interlude of withdrawal into isolationism following the

First World War, it was not until after the Second World War that the time seemed to have come to convert a military victory into a political and institutional one. It was only in Japan that the USA was unable to resist such a temptation. Even then, there was considerable resistance to too much imposition and for specialists, such as Robert Ward for Japan or Carl J. Friedrich for Germany, American intervention in creating a democratic order went much too far (cf. Chapter 1). The evolving antagonism with the ideologically doctrinaire Soviet Union strengthened the temptation for the USA to indulge in the same degree of ideological patronage in its own sphere of influence. At this point in time, however, it was, once again, the voice of caution that was heard most loudly – the voice of those opposed to answering Soviet uniformity with an ideological and institutional uniformity in the Western world.

Since America had no theory to export, there were many who believed that it should not try to export its political institutions either. The sociological approach to self-analysis (discussed in the Introduction) also had the effect of contributing to avoiding the narrow institutionalism (such as that shown by waves of adoptions of particular institutions in Europe) and remained sceptical regarding the transplantation of institutions into a different social environment.

It is a paradox of America's role as an example for others that its effectiveness as a model has become weaker, the stronger the country has become as a world power. The democratic creed began to jar increasingly with the interests of an imperial America, aiming to maintain the worldwide status quo. The strength of a Goliath began to be superimposed on the ideals of a David.[9] In this dilemma, it became common to draw daring parallels with Ancient Rome. Once again, a small agricultural state with a spartan life-style had made its way up to become the richest and most powerful state in the world in a short lapse of time. Toynbee saw the parallel between Rome and America in the loss of the role of an 'inspirer and leader of the World Revolution':

'America . . . now stands for what Rome used to stand for. In all the territories which fell under its influence, Rome always supported the rich against the poor . . . Lafayette is ready to pay a high psychological price in being transformed into a Metternich'[10]

These lines were written long before Kissinger boasted the role of a 'Metternich redivivus'. The parallel implied that, like Rome, America was drawn all too abruptly into a worldwide commitment, which overstretched its resources:

'Like Rome, the United States, once involved, have found it easier to steer clear of avowed opponents of freedom in power than to lead all their

119

allies and friends into ambiguous situations – with their controlling economy which commands respect without allowing the sort of risk to arise which could get out of hand'[11]

America did not have the advantage of close federal ties with dependent allies that Rome did. George Liska hoped that the 'American constitutional models' could turn out to be an equivalent.[12] Nonetheless, the daring parallel did show that there are lasting alliances, however much the one between America and Europe needed to be repeatedly defended against the charge of not having an historical basis.[13] But such historic parallels conceal the fact that, precisely because the American influence was weaker than that exerted in past empires, such alliances are presumably more durable, since they are more strongly supported by a consensus in the nations concerned.

Radical left-wing critics of America's role as a model do not see that side of America's world power policy which brings about a consensus, but only the 'self-justification as a matter of course', the 'absence of an awareness for injustice' and a 'syndrome of political blindness'. It must be admitted that the evidence for this line of argument is taken predominantly from the policy towards Latin America – one which is aimed much less at establishing consensus. This particular view would claim that America's expansion at the expense of Spain, France and Great Britain, which, in the nineteenth century remained unatoned imperialism, created an imbalanced, ethnocentric view of history which 'had the function of establishing an ideological justification for the implementation of unilateral interests.'[14] Compared with the Soviet Union, that will need to be seen in more differentiated terms. We are, however, still left with the dilemma, that, on the one hand, the bombastic support for the extension of democracy surfaces in such highly problematical cases as Carter's human rights campaign against the Soviet Union, while, on the other hand, a show of particular connivance and tolerance is displayed vis-à-vis allied authoritarian regimes. Whereas magnanimity in dealing with the former wartime enemies was a positive factor, it lost much of its value when similar magnanimity was displayed towards regimes from Spain to South Vietnam, whose internal order still bore all the characteristics of the defeated powers of 1945. The repercussions of such compromises between ideals and institutions in foreign policy have been overestimated, especially at the time of the Vietnam War. There was no domestic move towards Fascism in America. The erroneous forecast had, however, immunized itself against being disproved in advance by postulating a specific American form of Fascism:

'The specific feature of an American-type fascist development would most probably mean that deep structural crises would not, or at least not to any great extent, generate politically organized alternative movements in America, such as would represent a serious challenge to the ruling social class . . . the absence of such alternative mass-movements admittedly has the effect of making open fascist terror or unconstitutional seizure of power objectively superfluous, or, at least, highly unlikely but, on the other hand, it facilitates the creeping transition to the fascist-like methods and stabilization techniques which are immanent in the system. . .'[15]

Left-wing and conservative analysts all agree that there is an opposition in America which is strongly bound to the American credo and from which no fundamental threat to the system is to be expected. One conservative observer, Huntington, goes even further: 'The only thing that pushes extremist movements into an extreme position is the basic underlying mood in their own society.'[16]

The conclusions drawn from this finding however, point in opposite directions. It is precisely because the opposition is only fundamental insofar as it appeals for a return to the 'fundamentals' of the democratic credo that the result was not creeping Fascism but rather a democratic self-purification of the system. It happens much less frequently in America than in Europe that opponents are discredited with the accusation of wanting a 'completely different type of republic'. Since the American institutions are weaker than European ones, they are more sensitive to pressure from below than are European bureaucracies. It is hard to imagine how little actually changed in France despite the turbulent student revolution of 1968. In bureaucratic systems, opportunities for reform are rarely institutionalized and they tend (as in the case of France) to take the shape of revolutionary outbreaks.

Given such a surprising degree of evolution in a relatively open political system, the image of America has also undergone a rapid change. For a while, it appeared that a worldwide wave of anti-Americanism might have discredited the American model for good. The type of interpretation placed on it – along the lines of 'Pentagonism', 'imperialism', or 'military–industrial complex' – overshadowed the democratic model that America had once represented. The 'American model' became negative. The handful of Conservative voices protesting the opposite could hardly be heard above the tidal wave of anti-American utterances.

Appearances were deceptive. Contrary to the case of nineteenth-century Liberals, it was America's *policy* that was rejected. The model of *society*, on the other hand, still retained a certain degree of validity. In America itself there was a widespread failure to understand that the rejection of the USA applied only to its role as world policeman. Surveys carried out in the countries of the European Community into the trustworthiness of other people showed that the Americans came out better than all the major European nations. They were only outclassed by smaller peoples, such as the Swiss, the Luxemburgers and the Dutch, who had not unleashed any serious conflict for many centuries and who thus qualified to remain 'everybody's darling' (cf. Table 6.1). American society still has sufficient appeal to make it appear as a viable alternative to an individual's homeland. Whereas Jefferson once said of France that everyone has two home countries, his own and France, then as far as the élites of Europe are concerned, such a statement applies much more to America than it ever did to France. It is true that when France still acted as a model, the élite of other countries used to speak French, eat French and dress French – but only a small section of the élite felt at home there. America with its open society has offered cultural and economic élites the opportunity offered by no model country before, of spending a period of time as 'temporary Americans'. The 'Atlantic oligarchy', once forecast by Servan-Schreiber[17], has, however, not yet resulted. The patterns of recruitment to the élite and the styles of leadership among European élites are still too disparate for that to happen.

The criticism of American policy among sections of European youth cannot simply be taken as anti-Americanism, since it is perfectly compatible with admiration for the American way of life. In Germany, where, since the student revolt and the ecological protest movement, many Americans have suspected the presence of 'ungrateful', reckless anti-Americanism, young people, in particular, when asked what nation they would choose if they were not Germans, answered as the average nationalistic American would expect: if the hypothetical case were to materialize, most of them would prefer to be US citizens. On the other hand, the majority of Americans also maintained a strong orientation towards Europe, even if they regarded it as hopelessly divided and incapable of defending itself. At the peak of the Eurocommunist wave which was frequently misinterpreted as Moscow's fifth column, 49 per cent of Americans came down in favour of America exerting economic and political pressure in the event of a Communist takeover and 22 per cent even favoured American military intervention[18].

A more discriminating view of the image America developed among left-wing circles would prefer the term 'a-Americanism' rather than 'anti-Americanism'. For some time, the left-wing intelligentsia then had very little to do with America, and other favoured countries tended to attract attention. Before the Second World War, this was often the Soviet Union; later on Cuba and China appeared more attractive.[19] For the most radical Maoist factions all that was left in the end was the small country of Albania, because 'true Socialism' appeared to have been undermined by 'revisionism' everywhere else. A somewhat more modest

Table 6.1: Trust in other people
(Mean values of answers given in the EC countries)

	very trustworthy	fairly trustworthy	not part. trustworthy	not trustworthy	don't know	total	confidence index
Americans	24%	43%	16%	8%	9%	100%	0.47
Belgians	15	46	13	4	22	100	0.54
British	13	46	22	9	10	100	0.29
Chinese	13	19	12	27	29	100	-0.23
Danish	17	41	10	4	28	100	0.62
Dutch	19	43	11	5	22	100	0.58
French	14	39	23	13	11	100	0.17
Germans (Fed. Rep.)	18	42	17	12	11	100	0.32
Greeks	6	32	24	11	27	100	0.02
Irish	10	35	19	10	26	100	0.17
Italians	5	32	31	18	14	100	-0.23
Japanese	15	33	19	14	19	100	0.15
Luxembourgers	15	41	11	4	29	100	0.59
Portuguese	5	28	25	12	30	100	-0.11
Russians	4	16	23	41	16	100	-0.61
Spaniards	7	34	29	13	17	100	-0.17
Swiss	30	41	9	5	15	100	0.68

Source: Euro-Barameter 14 (including Greece)

123

wave of revolutionary tourism was triggered in Portugal in the mid-seventies and in Nicaragua in the early eighties. Increasingly, however, the political pilgrims showed the same signs of disappointment that one-time fans of America had done. Their support for the country of their predilection only rarely meant the hope of finding a model for their own country. An uneventful existence in the Neckar Valley had more of a motivating effect than did Utopian hopes triggered by the communes in the Tejo Valley. It was possible to demonstrate solidarity without actually fighting in a 'Spanish Civil War' as thousands of left-wing political pilgrims had done before the Second World War. Even among those subscribing to Marxist thought, the idea of finding a ready-made model of Socialism in a real-life situation was treated with increasing scepticism by left-wing intellectuals. The greater discrimination shown by neo-Marxist thought has led especially to greater moderation in the verdict given on the American model.

Even where there was no abatement in anti-Americanism, it would be wrong to overestimate its true scope. There is a form of anti-Americanism in politics which goes hand-in-hand with adopting most aspects of the American way of life – a combination satirized in the following lines:[20]

> 'He sat there,
> Wearing Farmer's trousers,
> Cursing the Americans.
> In the background:
> The roar of rock-and-roll.
> I said:
> Spit out that gum,
> So I can understand you better.
> He replied: Okay!'

The passing of judgement on America from a more aloof position has been a recurring phenomenon. What was new, however, was the speed with which the American model stopped being purely on the defensive. A further circumstance was helpful in this process, namely, that once the neo-Marxist waves had ebbed, America now for the first time had an ideology to offer: neo-conservatism. Until then, all concepts of government intervention ever since the New Deal had been imported from Europe into America. The countermovement of denationalization appeared to help American ideologies to make their first-ever breakthrough. One exponent of the moderate Left, Jürgen Habermas, tried to find the positive aspects of what had been adopted from America:

Political culture in the Federal Republic of Germany would be in a far

124

worse position today, had it not taken up and assimilated impulses from the American political culture in the decades immediately following the War. For the first time in German history, the Federal Republic opened itself to Western influences without reservation; at that time we adopted the political theory of the enlightenment; we grasped the power to mould mentalities that was contained in that pluralism originally propagated by religious sects; we became acquainted with the radical democratic spirit of American pragmatism from Pierce through to Mead and Dewey.[21]

Despite the American influences, the Frankfurt philosopher expressed his fears of the danger of a 'relapse' into daydreaming about a particular 'German way', where very little would remain of democracy apart from the constitutional state. My view here is that it is the opposite which appears to be more noteworthy: the reason that German neo-conservatism was able to learn so much from its American counterpart (and to maintain its distance vis-à-vis the intellectually strong *nouvelle droite* in France, which was more inclined towards the old Weimar traditions) was *inter alia* because neo-conservatism went through a process of both modernization and 'Americanization'. It became technocratic and abandoned its former organicism and irrationalism. The inclination that certain neo-conservatives showed for populist mobilization was a thorn in the flesh of many conservatives of the old school.[22] Nonetheless, the influence of American neo-conservatism with its anti-welfare state component is still only limited in those countries where a Christian Democratic party represents the strongest non-socialist political force. Not all the ideas taken over from America since the 'change in tack' can be lumped together as uniform neo-conservative theory. The pragmatic-eclectic ideas that came from America to Europe have not developed into a uniform theory of neo-conservatism there either. The extent to which American-style neo-conservatism is capable of propagation is also exaggerated on occasions. Since social democracy and reformist liberalism have been forced onto the defensive, neo-conservatism has no longer experienced sufficient opposition to sustain it, and its very victory has also represented its ideological demise.[23]

With the growth of the freedom movement in Europe, new forms of anti-Americanism have emerged and it is they that are having a negative effect on the American image today. From America's point of view, it has proved to be detrimental that the unorthodox Left no longer regards the Soviet Union as a serious threat. The less flexible the perception of Soviet immobilism, the less tolerant is the reaction to American dominance in Western Europe. The term 'Finlandization' is now being applied to America's relations with its allies.[24] The illusion that there are two symmetrical hegemonies is spreading: for the de-Sovietization of Eastern Europe to become possible, Western Europe must be de-Americanized. Sometimes that is taken to mean not only the reduction in American hegemony but also psychological de-Americanization as well. The psychologist, Horst Eberhard Richter addressed a peace conference of the 'International Physicians for the Prevention of Nuclear War' towards the end of 1985, and, speaking of the Germans, he said: 'We have remained the intellectual semi-Americans that we became in 1945'. Speaking in an interview, Jürgen Habermas took the same theory to an extreme when he said: 'The Federal Republic has become the fifty-second state of America to such an extent that all we are still lacking is American electoral law.'[25]

Conservatives, on the other hand, see peace as being guaranteed not through intellectual distance vis-à-vis America but by intellectual distance vis-à-vis the Soviet Union: 'Pragmatic reasoning on how best to avoid war' seems all the more likely to be successful, 'the less it is burdened with the impassioned activities of ideological bridge-builders.'[26] Unfortunately, this view is not without its justification. Conservative governments have often had it easier in their dealings with Moscow than have liberal ones.[27] Innocent goodwill has often gone unrewarded by the other side.

Left-wing and 'alternative' dreams about de-Americanization concentrate their criticism above all on America's military and economic dominance. There was, however, a current of critical theory which followed the spirit of the old Frankfurt school and Marcuse, which held America to be the incarnation of all aspects of technocratic, bureaucratic and colonial developments throughout the living world. Compared with the other superpower, this particular view sees, above all else, a negative convergence on the terrain of a technocratic society. Modern left-wing cultural criticism is beginning to establish pionts of contact with the older right-wing cultural criticism of Spengler and Keyserling.

Having lost its world-power positions after the Second World War, Europe was still able to console itself with the 'Athens complex'. Just like the ancient Athenians felt vis-à-vis Rome, Europe regarded itself as the refuge of 'true culture'. It is precisely this cultural comparison between Rome and America that misses the mark drastically – Rome did not possess the scientific and technological leadership that America has now achieved.[28] Cultural hegemony is very often the focal point for criticism from both Left and Right. The assumption is frequently made that there is a dearth of 'higher culture' in America, as if that country were still populated only by the hillbillies, whom a conservative aristocrat, Chateaubriand, once excused in the following condescending terms: 'Staying alive must come before thinking.' Such contemptuous attitudes have still not died out. A German art historian recently reached new depths when he maintained that the high numbers of American tourists in Europe were due to alienation from their own non-culture:

126

The decisive point here is that our big cities are becoming more and more American but the Americans pour in their droves into our small towns, which are still more or less intact. The reason is that it is here where they still feel relatively at ease and stimulated. In Venice, Salzburg, Innsbruck, Munich, Lucerne or Florence it is impossible to move for Yankees at the height of the season. This cannot be due only to a need for art and culture. It represents a dissatisfaction with the world that they have created for themselves and which their tragic blinderedness still leads them to regard as the best of all possible worlds. In their heart of hearts they don't really like their surrogate world at all, because, in the final analysis, all that it contains is sensationalism and a hollow ring transmitted by means of hypocritical phraseology. And that quite simply is not enough to present it to other peoples as an example for the world to follow.[29]

If this thesis were correct, then the argument would rebound on the Germans: why, in *per capita* terms, are they still ahead of the Americans in the world-travel league table? Only to satisfy a need for art and culture?

It is rare for so many anti-American caricatures to be lumped together in such a blatant form in a single sentence. Among genuine connoisseurs of international culture, the word has got around that America has produced a very rich literature. The fact that America has increasingly taken over the leadership in the fine arts and music has gone unnoticed. Sometimes this is also repudiated, such as by the author just quoted, who speaks of 'the only architectural achievement of merit produced in this melting pot of peoples' since the Chicago school as being in the process of collapse and who regarded the *Bauhaus* emigrants in America as stunted in their creativity. Generally speaking, cultural hegemony is seen as being restricted to the realm of what is considered to be a second-rate entertainment culture. There can be no doubt that it is in this area that the most spectacular advance in the USA's world reputation has been made. It does not even stop at the borders of the Soviet Empire, which claims to have developed an immeasurably superior 'Socialist life-style', but which is *de facto* becoming increasingly penetrated by Westernized American patterns of culture among its young people. The Soviet leadership still generally perceives this as 'deviant behaviour' and, significantly, attaches the English term 'hooliganism' (*chuliganstvo*) to it.

Although the star of the American model of democracy may have faded somewhat, America's society, economy and technology have become much more influential than even the most pessimistic prophets of the nineteenth century, beginning with Tocqueville, could ever have foreseen. But priorities have shifted. Whereas, in those days, it was customary to praise the political institutions and to reject social developments, today it is very often the opposite that applies.

It is possible to choose from among a plethora of depravation theories forecasting the demise of American democracy – not least by American writers themselves. Fortunately the crisis mongerers are unable to agree amongst themselves. This is most striking in the case of contributions to the Trilateral Commission on the 'Crisis of Democracy', a book that has been highly instrumental in propagating the thesis of the ungovernability of modern democracies. In his chapter on the USA, Huntington expressed the fear that democracy could represent its own worst enemy: 'Democracy is a greater threat to itself in the United States than in Europe or Japan, where residual inheritances of traditional and aristocratic values still remain alive'.[30]

Although the authors were given the opportunity to coordinate their forecasts to some extent, Crozier came to exactly the opposite conclusion for Europe: rapid social evolution is eroding the traditional modes of social control in society and precisely because of that it is endangering democracy: 'It is an area where Europe is much more vulnerable than either the United States or Japan.'[31] The only thing the two authors agree on is their euphoric view of Japan's future prospects, despite the fact that the Japanese themselves take a much more cautious view of the situation, given the erosion of traditional values and patterns of behaviour. This example does, however, serve to show that even modern scientific rationality is unable to get by entirely without cultural–pessimistic myths and idealized lands somewhere far away. In some ways, the broad brush analyses have made no progress since Tocqueville's day.

There is hardly a model country that has led to so many erroneous forecasts, and Huntington adjusted his view a few years later with a somewhat more optimistic interpretation of what could happen in America. It is precisely the decline in the confidence shown in the country's leadership and institutions (which was once seen as a dangerous sign of crisis) that he now maintains to be America's strength. The tension created by the 'ideals versus institutions' gap ('IvI') appears to have the effect of producing new ideas. The cyclic renaissance in the American democratic credo produces a periodic effect whereby revolts against the current forms of exercise of power lead to their purification. The legitimacy of the American government is now seen as being inversely proportional to belief in the American ideals.[32]

Does America still have its old special role when it comes to its regenerative capability? This is an area where the American model has had virtually no influence on Europe. It does appear at first sight as if similar processes of self-purification are developing in all the Western democracies, once the burdens represented by the relics of older rigidly structured societies and the fragmentation of society have diminished. The new social movements representing the biggest challenge to the

Western democracies today profess a much greater allegiance to the basic consensus than do the older movements and parties from which they emerged, whereby all they are doing is standing up for democratic ideals in a more radical manner than the Establishment, which has been turning something of a blind eye. It is still common to accuse opponents of wanting to set up 'a completely different type of republic' but such assertions are generally becoming increasingly difficult to believe. All the Western democracies are developing the ability to reintegrate fundamental oppositions into the system – something that has always been one of America's strong points.

America does, however, still maintain its special role as far as foreign policy is concerned, and it is doubtful whether similar repair mechanisms can repeatedly bridge the gap between ideals and institutions here. Which are the institutions that would be capable of regenerating world policy ideals? Is it not the case that American ideals themselves are repeatedly a source of contention in foreign policy? No country in history has been cosseted so much by its successes as has America. No country has ever had to pay so little for its mistakes, since no country has so far been able to represent a serious threat to America in its own hemisphere. This type of historical experience and the particular American cultural and religious traditions, the touchstone of which is rapid success coupled to instant rewards (irrespective of whether they are expected of the market, politics or God,[33] have the effect of strengthening certain characteristics of that very self-justification that can turn the ideals into a threat. A number of sociologists are beginning to doubt whether America actually possesses that ability to learn which was forced upon countries like France, Italy, Germany or Japan as a consequence of their defeats.

The processes of revolt engendered by fundamentalist values, which appear to guarantee a period of regeneration in domestic policy, have no equivalent in American international policy. Institutions embracing the whole world are losing their insignificance since America started the process of gradual withdrawal from the UN and its specialized agencies. Once upon a time, the United Nations Organization was the favourite child of Roosevelt's ideas for a new world order. Today the UN can, at best, be seen as a child taken into care and one for which decency alone still dictates the payment of maintenance. Since the USA's position of hegemony has been on the decline, it has been necessary in the Western world either to create completely new institutions or to instil a spirit of two-way cooperation into existing ones. Whereas, at the time of the Vietnam War, American involvement was portrayed as a deliberate, concentrated imperialist process in sharp contrast to the old thesis of the USA as a 'world power despite itself', the present-day theoretical discussion of international relations would tend rather to suggest the decline of American hegemony. Hegemony appears to be the product of a major war and, hence, not something that it is possible to maintain throughout lengthy periods of peace.[34] Dangers are sensed not so much in an excess of hegemony but in its erosion.[35] The latent longing of a number of American theoreticians and active politicians to 'return to a state of hegemony' is countered by more thoughtful analysts such as Robert Keohane with the demand for forms of cooperation to replace hegemony and the development of multilateral institutions.[36]

A more optimistic interpretation of America's worldwide reputation has become possible since the fall from favour of the old theory, which concentrated on structures of states' military power in a sort of billiard-ball model, where they only touched each other at the edges. The interdependence theory, as developed in America, tends, on the other hand, to see the world as an asymmetrical network of interactions and mutual dependencies. Former hegemonic powers, such as America, are also not immune to displaying signs of sensitivity (for example through the oil-price shock of 1973) and vulnerability (for instance, through protests such as the anti-Vietnam War movement in America). It is also possible for social contagion effects and growing transnational communications to increase the sensitivity of former hegemonic powers in the same way as political and economic interdependencies can. This approach views the situation as being characterized less by the unilateral decline of America's power and more by the decline in hierarchy as a world system.[37] If this view is the correct one, then the cards in America's hand are by no means as bad as is often assumed in Europe.

At first sight, alienation appears to be a continuing process within the Western system. Attempts have been made in Europe, and especially in Germany, to establish the existence of a successor generation showing neutralist and anti-American inclinations and tending towards preferring to maintain the same distance vis-à-vis both world powers.[38] Overhasty critics on the American side of the Atlantic are reacting with the threat of 'withdrawing their affection' and moving the focus of their attention into the Pacific hemisphere. Criticisms of a new obscureness and unpredictability in Europe are countered by European observers appealing for a clearer leadership stance. They also criticize rapid fluctuations in American policy: one day, it takes the form of a call for an embargo against the Soviet Union, the next, it indulges in profitable grain sales to Moscow.[39]

Even pro-American observers of that country's foreign policy are demanding 'a greater degree of political consistency'.[40] What is more important than calls to order (which are justified in themselves), however, is the willingness to draw conclusions from an analysis of the actual state of changes in the world's makeup and the decline of hegemonic power. A factor in favour of the influence of the American model is the increasing importance of economic, cultural and communicative processes. Anti-Americanism also still has much too much of a fixation on attempts to establish a military balance. The often rather obtuse debate surrounding contemporary forms of hegemony (actually, the term 'international leadership' is the only one used – so that no one will feel hurt) pays too little attention to the fact that the Soviet Union's hegemony within its own bloc is also threatened by trends which could lead to its delayed but nonetheless lasting erosion. The main danger here is that, for ideological reasons, the Soviet Union will be less inclined to accept a partial diminution in its power than America, and a belief in the expansion of the worldwide socialist camp will lead it to experiments in parts of the Third World where big-power influence is less well structured. This, in turn, could bring it into confrontation with America. To date, the Soviets have, however, avoided any form of direct confrontation, preferring to rely on victory coming more from the ideological class struggle. This, however, is also a particular area where America's exemplary role is highly vulnerable but where it has always been able to recover to such an extent that the attractiveness of the Soviet model has declined drastically in the more highly developed democratic systems. Even the Soviet Union itself is being dragged into the current of interdependencies. To begin with, the Conference on Security and Cooperation in Europe (CSCE) appeared to represent a victory for the Soviet Union, but before it fully recognized the fact, it found itself in the course of the later conferences increasingly cast less in the role of public prosecutor and more in the role of the accused in matters of human-rights violations.

Any appeal made today for America to show a greater degree of consistency in its leadership can no longer really afford to ignore the other Superpower. The American Superpower's relative loss of power within its sphere of influence can only be tolerated if accompanied by a similar reduction in the power of the Soviet Union within its own bloc, so that the perception of mutual threat remains reasonably symmetrical in both countries. We are, however, still some distance away from that state of affairs. Despite repeated attacks on America's 'arrogance of power', a comparison with the Soviet Union has shown that the American élite has a greater ability to assess the other side with realism or even with empathy. Self-justification and ideological dogmatism are even greater on the Soviet side. Although an empirical investigation into the degree of mismatch between self-perception and perception of the other side estimates a ratio of 11:4 in favour of the USA,[41] it should be added, by way of a rider, that this type of image analysis is based primarily on verbally expressed attitudes, and that these tend to deviate more from actual attitudes in the Soviet Union than in the USA.

Ever since the early nineteenth century, comparisons have been made between the two territorially vast countries, USA and Russia, and if there is to be a narrowing of the internal differences between them, then that could cause nightmares for certain Europeans. Paul Watzlawick was going completely against the grain when he decided to suppress the vision he had:

> What, indeed, will be the outcome, if it ever happens that the two giants, sandwiched between which is Europe wiling away its impotent existence, should ever become aware of their similarity, for instance the way they are both torn to and fro between brutal big-power ideas and threadbare ethical or ideological trimmings? But such a nightmare has no place in a travel anthology, so let us suppress it once again in our subconscious minds.[42]

Anyone less inclined to rush into premature theories of convergence will prefer to pin their hopes on domestic policy having a stronger influence on foreign policy, displaying that American ability to dismantle any self-justified exercise of power by an appeal for a return to basic American ideals. That is only likely if the decline in the USA's power does not take on too drastic a form. Replacing hegemony with a more mutual form of cooperation would certainly do no harm at all to the exemplary role of the American model. Investigations have shown that America's role as a model was at its most secure during periods when America was neither too weak nor too strong.

Notes

1   Robert Wesson: *Democracy in Latin America. Promise and Problems*, New York, Praeger, 1982, pp. 83ff.
2   H. von Holst: *Verfassung und Demokratie der Vereinigten Staaten von Amerika*, Düsseldorf, Buddeus, 1873, Vol. 1, p. 57.
3   Bradford Smith: *The American Character:* Institute for International Educations. New Bulletin, 1958, No. 1 (58-67), pp. 66f; Jürgen Gebhardt: *Die Krise des Amerikanismus*, Stuttgart, Klett, 1976, p. 224, p. 271; Bernard Crick: *The American Science of Politics*, Berkeley, University of California Press, 1967, p. 8.
4   Knud Krakau: *Missionsbewusstsein und Völkerrechtsdoktrin in den Vereinigten Staaten von Amerika*, Frankfurt, Metzner, 1967, pp. 23ff.
5   Talcott Parsons: *Authority, Legitimation and Political Action*, in: Carl J. Friedrich (ed): *Authority*. Cambridge/Mass., Harvard UP, 1958 (197-221) p. 199.
6   Daniel J. Boorstin: *The Genius of American Politics*, Chicago UP, 1956, p. 134.
7   John C. Calhoun: *Works*, ed. Richard K. Crall, New York, 1888, Vol. 4, p. 416.
8   Raymond Aron: *Die imperiale Republik*, Stuttgart, Belser, 1975, pp. 38ff.
9   Robert A. Isaak: *American Democracy and World Power*, New York, St. Martins Press, 1977, p. 189.

10   Arnold Toynbee: *America and the World Revolution*, London, Oxford UP, 1962, pp. 16f.
11   George Liska: *Imperial America: The International Politics of Primacy*, Baltimore, John Hopkins Press, 1967, p. 24.
12   Liska, op. cit. p. 25.
13   Karl Kaiser: *Die europäische Herausforderung und die USA*, Munich, Piper, 1973, p. 200.
14   Ekkehart Krippendorff: *Die amerikanische Strategie*, Frankfurt, Suhrkamp, 1970, p. 445.
15   Krippendorff, op. cit., p. 457.
16   Samuel P. Huntington: *American Politics. The Promise of Disharmony*, Cambridge/Mass, Belknap, 1981, p. 36.
17   Jean-Jacques Servan-Schreiber: *Le défi américain*, Paris, Denoël, 1967, p. 211.
18   *Allensbacher Jahrbuch der Demoskopie 1979-1983*. Vol. 8, Munich, Saur, 1983, p. 190; J. Robert Schaetzel: *Das Europabild der Amerikaner*, in: Karl Kaiser/ Hans-Peter Schwarz (eds.): *Amerika und Westeuropa*, Stuttgart, Belser, 1977, (29-40), p. 32.
19   Paul Hollander: *Political Pilgrims. Travels of Western Intellectuals to the Soviet Union, China and Cuba*, Oxford UP, 1981.
20   Bernard Katsch, cited in: *Kurt Tudyka: Anti-Amerikanismus – was ist das?* in: Anton-Andreas Guha/Sven Papcke (eds): *Amerika – der riskante Partner*, Königstein, Athenäum, 1984 (117-130), p. 129.
21   Jürgen Habermas: Die Kulturkritik der Neokonservativen in den USA und in der Bundesrepublik. Über eine Bewegung von Intellektuellen in zwei Kulturen, *Merkur*, 1982, No. 11 (1047-1061), p. 1061.
22   Jan van Houten: *Ideen haben Folgen. Die konservative Bewegung in Amerika*, Criticon, No. 73/73, 1982 (155-160), p. 160; Hans Rühle et al. (eds.): *Der Neo-Konservatismus in den Vereinigten Staaten und seine Auswirkungen auf die Atlantische Allianz*, Melle. Knoth, 1982, p. 10.
23   Jakob Schissler (ed.): *Neokonservatismus in den USA*, Opladen, Westdeutscher Verlag, 1983, p. 165.
24   Régis Debray: *Les Empires contre l'Europe*, Paris, Gallimard, 1985, p. 58.
25   Frankfurter Rundschau, 4.11.1985, Jürgen Habermas: *Die neue Unübersichtlichkeit*, Frankfurt, Suhrkamp, 1985, pp. 217f.
26   Hermann Lübbe, In: Rühle, op. cit. p. 103.
27   Gebhard Schweigler: *Von Kissinger zu Carter. Entspannung im Widerstreit von Innen- und Aussenpolitik*. 1969-1981, Munich, Oldenbourg, 1982, p. 491.
28   Max Lerner: *America as a Civilisation*, New York, Simon & Schuster, 1957, p. 935.
29   Chateaubriand: *Mémoires d'outre tombe*, Paris, Flammarion, 1982 (Book 8, Ch. 10), p. 345; Hans Koepf: *Stadtbaukunst*, Sigmaringen. Thorbecke, 1985, p. 10.
30   Michel Crozier et al: *The Crisis of Democracy*, New York, UP, 1975, p. 114.
31   Ibid, p. 24.
32   Huntington, op. cit., p. 41.
33   Michel Crozier: *The Trouble with America*, Berkeley, University of California, 1984, p. 75.
34   Robert Gilpin: *War and Change in World Politics*, Cambridge UP 1981, pp. 210ff.
35   Charles Kindleberger: Dominance and Leadership in the International Economy. *International Studies Quarterly*, 1981, pp. 242-254.
36   Robert O. Keohane: *After Hegemony. Cooperation and Discord in the World Political Economy*, Princeton UP, 1984, pp. 182ff.

37   Robert O. Keohane/Joseph S. Nye: *Power and Interdependence. World Politics in Transition*, Boston. Little Brown, 1977, pp. 12f, 228.
38   Stephen F. Szabo (ed.): *The Successor Generation: International Perspectives of Postwar Europeans*, London, Butterworths, 1983, p. 70; Alan Platt (ed.): *The Atlantic Alliance. Perspectives from the Successor Generation*, Santa Monica, Rand Corporation, 1983.
39   Marion Gräfin Dönhoff: *Amerikanische Wechselbäder:* Stuttgart, DVA, 1983, p. 307; Peter Merseburger: *Die unberechenbare Vormacht. Wohin steuern die USA?* Munich, Bertelsmann, 1983, p. 272.
40   Gebhard Schweigler: *Grundlagen der aussenpolitischen Orientierung der Bundesrepublik Deutschland*, Baden-Baden, Nomos, 1985, p. 229.
41   Daniel Frei: *Feindbilder und Abrüstung. Die gegenseitige Einschätzung der UdSSR und der USA*, Munich, Beck, 1985, p. 133.
42   Paul Watzlawick: *Gebrauchsanweisung für Amerika*, Munich, Piper, 1984, 8th edn., p. 160.

Index